FIRST PEOPLES of NORTH AMERICA

THE PEOPLE AND CULTURE OF THE

HURON

RAYMOND BIAL

Cavendish
Square

New York

Published in 2016 by Cavendish Square Publishing, LLC
243 5th Avenue, Suite 136, New York, NY 10016

Copyright © 2016 by Cavendish Square Publishing, LLC

First Edition

Website: cavendishsq.com

This publication represents the opinions and views of the author based on his or her personal experience, knowledge, and research. The information in this book serves as a general guide only. The author and publisher have used their best efforts in preparing this book and disclaim liability rising directly or indirectly from the use and application of this book.

CPSIA Compliance Information: Batch #CW16CSQ

All websites were available and accurate when this book was sent to press.

Library of Congress Cataloging-in-Publication Data

Bial, Raymond.
The people and culture of the Huron / Raymond Bial.
pages cm. — (First peoples of North America)
Includes bibliographical references and index.
ISBN 978-1-5026-1008-9 (hardcover) ISBN 978-1-5026-1009-6 (ebook)
1. Wyandot Indians—History—Juvenile literature.
2. Wyandot Indians—Social life and customs—Juvenile literature. I. Title.
E99.H9B43 2016
973.04'97555—dc23
2015023720

Editorial Director: David McNamara
Editor: Kristen Susienka
Copy Editor: Nathan Heidelberger
Art Director: Jeffrey Talbot
Designer: Amy Greenan
Senior Production Manager: Jennifer Ryder-Talbot
Production Editor: Renni Johnson
Photo Research: J8 Media

The photographs in this book are used by permission and through the courtesy of: Hulton Archive/ND/Roger Viollet/Getty Images, front cover, Raymond Bail, back cover; LOOK Die Bildagentur der Fotografen GmbH/Alamy, 6; Raymond Bail, 8, 10-11, 13, 15, 24–25, 26, 30, 39, 41, 44, 55, 73, 74, 81; Encyclopaedia Britannica/UIG/Getty Images, 18; Kane, Paul/Art Gallery of Ontario, Toronto, Canada/Bridgeman Images, 28; Embleton, Ron/Look and Learn/Bridgeman Images, 33; Grasset de Saint-Sauveur, Jacques/Collection of the New-York Historical Society, USA/Bridgeman Images, 35; Jules-Ernest Livernois/Library and Archives Canada, 36; Jules-Ernest Livernois/Library and Archives Canada, 47; Alexander Erdbeer/Shutterstock.com, 49; Charles Edward/Beaver wars map.jpg/Wikimedia Commons, 62; Posnov/Getty Images, 64; Keith Naylor/Shutterstock.com, 66; Prisma/UIG via Getty Images, 70; Public Domain/Jules-Ernest Livernois/Groupe Huron-Wendat Wendake 1880.jpg/Wikimedia Commons, 75; Stott, W.R.S./Private Collection/Bridgeman Images, 76; ClassicStock/Alamy, 79; Mary Evans Picture Library, 82; Francis Vachon/Alamy, 91, 92, 98–99; FT/Alamy, 95; Stéphane Groleau/Alamy, 100; Bygone Collection/Alamy, 102; Wyandotte Nation, 105; Culture Club/Getty Images, 107; Public Domain/Tarhe from History of Columbus (1909).png/Wikimedia Commons, 109; Public DomainWilliam E. Connelley/William Walker (Wyandot leader).jpg/Wikimedia Commons, 110; Hal Beral/VWPics/Newscom, 111.

Printed in the United States of America

ACKNOWLEDGMENTS

This book would not have been possible without the generous help of a number of individuals and organizations that have devoted themselves to preserving the culture of the Huron. I would like especially to thank Mary Mandley at Sainte-Marie among the Hurons and Jamie Hunter at the Huron Indian Village for their gracious hospitality, including permission to make photographs at these wonderful sites in Midland, Ontario.

As always, I am very much indebted to Cavendish Square Publishing for guiding this book through to completion. I would like to thank my wife, Linda, and my children, Anna, Sarah, and Luke, especially for their help during our trip to Huronia in the forests and lakes of Ontario to make photographs for this book.

CONTENTS

A Huron woman sits in a longhouse at Fort Sainte Marie among the Hurons.

AUTHOR'S NOTE

At the dawn of the twentieth century, Native Americans were thought to be a vanishing race. However, despite four hundred years of warfare, deprivation, and disease, Native Americans have persevered. Countless thousands have lost their lives, but over the course of this century and the last the populations of Native tribes have grown tremendously. Even as America's First People struggle to adapt to modern Western life, they have also kept the flame of their traditions alive—the languages, religions, stories, and the everyday ways of life. An exhilarating renaissance in Native American culture is now sweeping the continent from coast to coast.

The First Peoples of North America books depict the social and cultural life of the major nations, from the early history of Native peoples in North America to their present-day struggles for survival and dignity. Historical and contemporary photographs of traditional subjects, as well as period illustrations, are blended throughout each book so that readers may gain a sense of family life in a tipi, a hogan, or a longhouse.

No single book can comprehensively portray the intricate and varied lifeways of an entire tribe, or nation. I only hope that young people will come away with a deeper appreciation for the rich tapestry of Native American culture—both then and now—and a keen desire to learn more about these first Americans.

The Huron homeland had many lakes and marshes that supported various wildlife.

CHAPTER ONE

The name Huron comes from the French word Hure, *meaning "boar."*

A CULTURE BEGINS

Long before Europeans called North America home, the continent was inhabited by groups of Native Americans. These groups differed from region to region. Each had their own beliefs, their own languages, and their own cultures. They created structured communities in which they taught their children the ways of their people and how to hunt, gather, and fish.

They respected the land and all the animals that roamed it. One of these Native groups was the Huron (HYUR-ahn). For centuries, they have existed and lived off the land. While their lives changed forever after the arrival of Europeans, they persisted. Today they continue to be an integral part of North American and Native American history. They carry on their ancestors' traditions, heritage, and culture, and are proud to be part of the Huron Nation.

The Huron Begin

Thousands of years ago, the ancestors of the Huron and other Native Americans journeyed over a strip of land that once linked Siberia and Alaska. Following the herds of shaggy bison and other wild animals, wandering bands spread south and eastward over the continent of North America. Eventually, around 500 CE, the Huron settled in eastern Canada in what is now southern Ontario. Their name comes from the French *hure*, meaning "boar." The term may refer to a hairstyle worn by some of the men—popularly known today as a Mohawk—in which the head is shaved except for a brush-like ridge along the center of the scalp. They called themselves **Wendat**, or Ouendat, meaning "Islanders" or "Dwellers on a Peninsula." The name may have come from their

The Huron built longhouses, which were large buildings with arched roofs.

belief that Earth was a great island carried on the back of a turtle.

For the next five hundred years, in what became known as the pre-**Iroquoian** period, the Huron lived by hunting, fishing, and gathering. Around 1000 CE, in the early Iroquoian period, they learned to raise corn. The additional food allowed people to gather in **palisaded** villages, where they lived in **longhouses**. Beginning around 1300, in the middle-Iroquoian period, the Huron began to plant sunflowers not only as a food but also for their oil. About a century later, in the late Iroquoian period, they first cultivated beans and squash as crops. During this time, warfare escalated among the Native peoples of the region, and the Huron began to locate their villages closer together to better defend themselves.

This military cooperation led to the formation of a formal alliance, when four tribes known as the Attignawantan (Bear People), Attigneenongnahac (Cord People), Tahontaenrat (Deer People), and Arendahronon (Rock People) established the Huron League, possibly in the early 1500s. Within a century, the alliance had grown to include between twenty thousand and forty-five thousand members living in sixteen to twenty-five villages, each with about two thousand inhabitants. This powerful union enabled the Huron to dominate a **swath** of fertile land, about 20 miles (32.2 kilometers) long and 35 miles (56.3 km) wide between Georgian Bay and Lake Simcoe. The Huron called their territory **Wendake** (Wen-DAH-kee), meaning "Land of the Wendat." The area later became known as **Huronia**.

It was once believed that the Huron settled in this northern region to avoid the Iroquois, who lived in what is now upstate New York. Although the Iroquoian-speaking Hurons shared a similar language and customs with the Iroquois, including living in longhouses, they often warred with their neighbors to the south. Yet, despite the bitterly cold winters, the geography of Huronia also suited the people. The light soils could

This is what part of a typical Huron village looked like.

be easily worked, and Huronia was nearly surrounded by water. People caught fish in abundance throughout the year. Huronia's location at the southern edge of the Canadian Shield, a bleak, rocky plain stretching to the Arctic, became pivotal for trade. Here, too, were the only suitable canoe routes to the north. **Algonquian** hunters who wandered the north country exchanged furs and hides and dried meat and fish for nuggets of copper, which the Huron acquired by trade with peoples living to the west at Sault Sainte Marie and Lake Superior. The Algonquians also needed stores of corn to get through the winter, along with tobacco and other goods, which the Huron could provide for them.

For hundreds of years, the Huron had prospered as farmers, growing corn, beans, and squash in clearings near their longhouses. As their harvests became more bountiful, they were able to sustain more people and began to form larger villages. Although settled as farmers, the Huron had to move when the light, sandy soil became exhausted—typically, every ten to twenty years. They also traded extra corn and other goods with the Algonquian. As their population increased, the Huron engaged in long-distance trade with their friends and organized warfare against their enemies.

The Huron enjoyed a strong alliance and a stable society, as well as a rich cultural life. They passed down their heritage by word of mouth, through a process called oral tradition. Men, women, and children knew stories about their people from much repetition and retelling. Here is a version of the creation story they told over many generations, as people gathered around the longhouse fire:

> Many years ago, when there was only air and water, a woman named Aataentsic (ah-TANT-sik) lived in the Sky World. There were forests, lakes, rivers, and fields in the Sky World, and people lived there as they do now upon Earth. However, one day, Aataentsic fell through a great hole in the Sky World and tumbled downward through the air.
>
> No one is certain why Aataentsic fell from the Sky World. Some people say she was tending to her cornfield and saw a bear. When her dog pursued the lumbering bear, Aataentsic went after her beloved pet. By accident, the bear stumbled and plunged into

The Huron told stories about Earth being carried on the back of a turtle.

the hole, followed by the dog. Aataentsic crept
to the edge of the hole and when she could see
neither the bear nor the dog, she jumped into
the abyss. Others say that her husband, who
was very ill, dreamed that if he ate the fruit of
a certain tree he would be cured. To reach the
fruit, Aataentsic had to cut down the tree, but
at the first swing of her ax, the tree split and
crashed through the floor of the Sky World,
leaving a **chasm**. Aataentsic told her husband
what had happened. She then returned to the
gaping hole and threw herself after the tree.

Aataentsic was heavy with child when she tumbled from the Sky World. A flock of swans recognized her plight and glided under her. Flying wing tip to wing tip, they made a feathery raft for her. However, there was no land on which they could set her down—only water below in which fish and other creatures swam. Aataentsic could neither fly nor swim for very long, and the swans did not know what to do with her. Finally, Turtle rose to the surface and called upon Beaver and all the other animals of the water. "Dive to the bottom and bring up soil," Turtle instructed. "Place the soil on my back." The animals did so, and an island grew on Turtle's back.

The swans gently placed Aataentsic on this island, and there she made her home. In time, she gave birth to two sons, Tawiscaron (da-WIS-ga-ron) and Youskeha (you-SKE-ha). As they grew up, however, the two brothers fought—Youskeha wielding the horns of a stag and Tawiscaron using the fruits of the wild rosebush as a weapon. On one occasion, Youskeha struck his brother so hard that his blood flowed over the land. Flint sprang up from the blood, and in the language of the Huron, this stone—which they chipped into points for arrows and spears—came to be called *tawiscara* in honor of the wounded brother.

The People and Culture of the Huron

Both brothers ruled over Earth as gods, wielding great power yet acting as opposing forces. Youskeha often helped the people to have a better life, while Tawiscaron became spiteful and brought only sorrow and death.

Europeans in North America

The Huron's culture changed after Europeans settled on their land. Their arrival signaled the dawn of a new era, one that would change their lives and culture forever.

As they explored North America, the French encountered many Native tribes. Some historians argue that the Huron were among the Iroquoian-speaking peoples that Jacques Cartier met while exploring the St. Lawrence River in the mid-1500s. The territory Cartier explored—near the present-day cities of Montreal and Quebec—was further east than Huronia. It is possible, however, that some Huron bands were living there at the time of Cartier's expedition, later migrating farther west.

In the early 1600s, the Huron entered into more permanent contact with the French. By this time, the Huron were a thriving people living in villages scattered over Huronia, a peninsula of rolling hills. This was a region of forests and lakes where men hunted and caught fish in abundance. The Huron were united in a political league, or **confederacy**, of four distinct nations. Within each nation, the Huron lived in fortified villages and in smaller villages and hamlets.

To. 2. Pag. 130.

Baguette

Natte ou espéce de tapis

la Cérémonie du Mariage

couvre sa tête de sa
couverture, et lors-
quelle veut bien
l'entretenir elle se
met a son seant
et lui permet de
s'asseoir sur le
pied de son lict.

A

Vieillard allant recevoir à la
porte de la Cabane la mariée
accompagnés de ses parens.

This illustration from 1703 shows how Europeans and the Huron formed fur trade agreements.

The People and Culture of the Huron

The Huron established friendly relations with French explorer Samuel de Champlain in 1609, after which they became the most active traders of all the Native peoples in what became known as New France. They adeptly served as middlemen between the French and the Native peoples of the Great Lakes region in a growing international trade in furs, notably beaver pelts.

Yet from the moment the Huron came into contact with the French, their way of life began to change. French explorers, traders, and missionaries arrived in Huronia over the next forty years and gradually formed a complex and ultimately destructive relationship with the Native people. The Huron prospered as traders, yet they also became dependent on European goods. They strongly resisted the zealous attempts of **Jesuit** missionaries to convert them, but the French also brought European diseases—notably measles and smallpox—against which the Huron had no resistance. Starting in the early 1630s, thousands of people died; entire villages within the confederacy perished. Many survivors, noting that the French did not succumb to these maladies, converted to Christianity, leading to bitter conflict with those who steadfastly embraced traditional beliefs.

The French provided written accounts of the Huron way of life in three documents: Samuel de Champlain's account of his winter in Huronia (1615–1616), Gabriel Sagard-Théobat's account of his winter **sojourn** (1623–1624), and the *Jesuit Relations* written during the years 1634 to 1650. The *Jesuit Relations* were annual reports written by Catholic missionaries of the Jesuit order, who were fervently attempting to convert the Huron. One of the best-known Jesuit missionaries was Father Jean de Brébeuf.

This became a tragic period, lasting barely a half-century, in which French and Huron alike struggled for survival through the deep snow and dark nights of the northern winters. In 1649 and 1650, weakened by deadly illnesses and internal conflict, the Huron were mercilessly attacked by the Iroquois and driven from their homeland.

By 1648, having trapped all the beaver in their own streams, the Iroquois had pushed into Huronia in search of new territory for trapping and hunting. In the ensuing battles, the Iroquois used guns they had acquired from the Dutch along the Hudson River. The Huron were no match against these weapons and suffered many defeats. By the spring of 1649, they abandoned their villages. Some were killed by war parties, but many were adopted by the Iroquois, who needed to strengthen their numbers.

Those who avoided capture and did not starve to death sought refuge with neighboring peoples. Many Huron joined the Petun, who shared a similar language and culture. They lived just west of Huronia along the southern shore of Georgian Bay, but they too were driven out by the Iroquois, who feared that they would take over the **fur trade**. For the next half-century, the eight hundred survivors, mostly the Petun (also called the Tionontsti and sometimes the Tobacco) lived near Lake Superior. A band of Potawatomi living near Green Bay, Wisconsin, also sheltered one group of Huron.

In 1701, the French encouraged these few remaining Huron to settle near Fort Pontchartrain at the present site of Detroit, Michigan. They began to trade with the English, who called them the **Wyandot**, from their original name of Wendat. They migrated over what are now the states of Michigan, Ohio, Wisconsin, and Illinois. During this time, the Wyandot took part in battles in the Great Lakes region of the United States. In 1763, they joined Pontiac's great alliance of Native peoples against the British, who planned to occupy the formerly French-controlled area. They later fought alongside the British against the American colonists during the Revolutionary War (1775–1783) and against the young United States in the War of 1812. Thereafter, they continued to face European settlement in both Canada and the United States. A few descendants still live around Detroit, but most eventually migrated to Oklahoma and now make their home on the Wyandotte **Reservation**.

In Canada, about three hundred Christianized Hurons survived the winter of 1649–1650 on Gahoendoe Island, now Christian Island, off the coast of Huronia. The following summer they settled under French protection on the Ile d'Orléans near Quebec City. Six years later they moved to the mainland. Known as the Huron-Wendat of Wendake, they were eventually granted a reserve, where they make their home today. Although they no longer speak their original language, they strive to sustain their identity as a people.

Connecting to the Land

For several hundred years, the Huron lived among the forests and lakes near the shores of Georgian Bay. The region, which could be easily crossed by foot in three or four days, was bounded on the east by Lake Simcoe, on the west by Nottawasaga Bay, and on the north by Matchedash Bay. These three magnificent bodies of water, along with rivers and marshes to the south, formed natural boundaries for Wendake.

Small lakes were scattered throughout much of this territory. The largest of these—now Cranberry Lake, Orr Lake, and Bass Lake—lay near its southern edge. Running cold and clear, streams and rivers laced the forests and fields, emptying into the shimmering lakes. The Huron briskly paddled their canoes throughout this territory and along the shores of Georgian Bay to trade corn with the French and Algonquians and to make war against the Iroquois and other enemies. Much of Wendake was enveloped by the bay's long, curving shoreline of shifting sands and rocks worn by the waves over thousands of years. Here, the huge expanse of water was broken only by an island, seemingly floating above the waves, or by fragments of pine-studded cliffs piercing its surface.

In stunning contrast, much of the interior was distinguished by the canopy of hardwoods—primarily maple, beech, and oak—that blanketed much of the region, blending with occasional stands of white birch, which provided bark for canoes. There were also basswood, ash, and elm, with which the Huron sheathed their longhouses. White pines sprung up in clearings, and other evergreens thrived in the moist, low ground. Cedars, which the Huron also used in building longhouses, took root in the many swamps that dotted the land.

Wendake abounded in wildlife: bears, deer, wolves, coyotes, foxes, wolverines, and lynxes. There were also beavers, otters, muskrats, porcupines, raccoons, fishers, woodchucks, rabbits, weasels, and minks, which the Huron hunted or trapped. The marshes and lakes also teemed with fish and fowl, especially ducks and geese—the flocks were so large they often blackened the skies—as well as trumpeter swans. The Huron hunted deer for their meat and hides. They also relished the greasy flesh of bears. They could trap just about any animal, but they often traded with the Algonquian, exchanging corn and food stores for dried meat and fish. In later years, they traded beaver pelts to the French in exchange for European goods.

Like other Native Americans, the Huron lived according to the cycle of the seasons. In the spring, the sap began to rise in the maple trees. They tapped the trees and boiled down the sap to make crumbly brown maple sugar. However, the Huron were primarily farmers. To the south lay rich soils, yet the Huron preferred the less fertile but loose soils in their territory. Although trees had to be cleared for fields, the sandy **loam** was easily worked with stone tools. When the soil had thawed, they dug with sticks and planted their corn, beans, and squash, which they called the three sisters, as well as sunflowers. In early summer, they gathered berries, and in the long, dry months of July and August, as ears of corn ripened on their stalks, they gathered wild blueberries growing thick on bushes in the forest shade.

In the autumn, as the foliage turned red, yellow, and orange, the corn leaves and stalks faded to tan, the squash matured, drying beans rattled in their shells, and the sunflowers began to wilt. Women harvested these crops and gathered nuts before the first arctic

Corn was a popular crop for the Huron tribes to grow.

The People and Culture of the Huron

winds swept down. Through the short days of the long winter, the snows grew deep. The rivers and lakes froze and seemingly vanished under the drifts. People settled around the orange glow of their fires, trudging short distances in snowshoes to hunt deer or to fish through the ice of a nearby lake. They also pulled toboggans and sleds over the snow. Both game and fish could be scarce during the hard winters, but the Huron had ample stores of corn and dried meat.

Regardless of the season, people found a way to survive. They used the land around them to build structures, make clothes, and provide food. This land was plentiful and something to which they showed great respect. It was where their ancestors had lived, and it was where they thought they would continue to live for generations to come.

Longhouses were tall buildings constructed from trees.

*They build their cabins
all of bark and make
them very substantial.*

—Jacques Charles
Sabrevois, 1718

BUILDING A CIVILIZATION

As the Huron developed, so too did their communities. They settled in particular areas for long stretches of time— sometimes as many as twenty years—respectfully using the land, the animals, and other resources to survive. With each generation came new opportunities, and soon the Huron had built a remarkable culture and a thriving civilization.

Villages

The Huron carefully located their villages near water and tillable soil. They did not live directly on the shore of Georgian Bay because of its poor

This painting from 1845 shows a Native American encampment on Lake Huron.

soil and strong northwesterly winds. Instead, they chose inland sites on elevated land, preferably a bluff, near streams or freshwater springs. Villages also had to be near forests for wood and building materials.

The Huron fortified many of their villages with walls, or palisades. To make the walls, men first sharpened the ends of cedar or pine logs and then placed the logs side by side in trenches, the sharp points thrusting upward. They lashed the logs together with saplings and piled soil against the base to form a sturdy barricade. To make the single entrance, they overlapped the ends of the walls slightly so that anyone entering or leaving the village had to turn a corner. This slowed enemies who tried to invade the village.

The People and Culture of the Huron

Instead of a gate or door, the entrance was protected by wooden bars. Inside the wall, the men built lookout towers and platforms reached by wooden ladders. If an attack was anticipated, they stacked rocks on the platforms to throw down on their enemies and stockpiled jars of water to put out any fires.

Within the palisade, there might be as many as forty longhouses, standing in rows, just a few feet apart, all facing northeast away from the prevailing winds. The village had a sweat lodge and a wigwam for the shaman, or medicine man. There were also storage pits and drying racks for animal hides, as well as workplaces for grinding corn, making pottery, and repairing canoes.

Buildings

Depending on the season and the activity, the Huron lived in different types of buildings, the most common being the longhouse. About 90 to 100 feet long (27.4 to 30.5 meters) and 20 to 30 feet (6.1 to 9.1 m) wide, the longhouse had a rectangular base and walls that curved to form a domed roof.

To build a longhouse, the men first constructed a wooden structure by lashing poles together. They sheathed the framework with sheets of elm or cedar bark tied down with saplings and wooden strips. Longhouses had no windows—only a low doorway at each end and holes in the roof to allow smoke from the cooking fires to drift out. There was usually a porch at the entrance where wood and food were stored. Inside there was a row of shallow fire pits, each about 20 feet (6.1 m) apart. Each fire pit served two families.

The Huron made all of their belongings, including beds, baskets, and clothing.

The Huron built raised platforms along each side of the longhouse. During the winter, people slept on the floor near the warmth of the fires and stored their goods on the platforms. During the summer, they slept outside or bunked on the wide shelves cushioned with animal hides. They hung carved wooden masks, snowshoes, weapons, and other belongings on the posts and inside walls. Otherwise they furnished their longhouses simply, with bark or husk floor mats, clay pots, baskets, and hollow logs in which corn was stored.

A single longhouse might shelter ten or more families. Usually, with as many as six members in each family, thirty-six to forty people lived in each longhouse. Withstanding downpours and blizzards, as well as baking sun, a longhouse lasted about eight to twelve years. Rebuilding the longhouse was usually a cooperative effort in which people from other villages gathered to help.

Family Life

Clans, as well as families, formed the social structure in every village. Huron society was based on a system of eight extended families, or clans: Turtle, Deer, Wolf, Hawk, Bear, Porcupine, Beaver, and Snake. Clans owned the cornfields and the longhouses. Each family had a place within the longhouse, yet people also had to cooperate and work together as clans. Extended families included aunts and uncles and grandparents. Known as *yentiokwa*, the clans shaped the daily governance of villages and tribes. All the people in a clan considered themselves related, even if they belonged to different Huron nations. People remained members of their clan for life, and all the children grew up as brothers and sisters. A large clan might occupy several longhouses in the village, and each clan was represented in the four nations. Since members considered themselves related to their kin in other nations, a strong bond existed among all Huron.

Each clan was led by a male chief. However, elders, known as clan mothers, commanded respect and were often consulted in decisions. Huron society was also matrilineal, which means people traced their descent—in both family and clan—through a female ancestor. A man was born into his mother's clan. When he grew up and married, he remained a member of his clan, but his children became part of their mother's clan. Managing the household was the exclusive domain of the women. The clan mother directed farming and the other daily tasks shared by the women in the village. Revered for her wisdom and experiences, she also helped settle disputes within the longhouse.

Leagues and Councils

The Huron were organized into four nations, or tribes, which constituted the Huron League. Although they shared a common language and hunting grounds, each of the four tribes lived in its own territory and governed through its own council. Each nation also followed its own customs and traced its own distinctive history. Living close together, the nations kept peace among themselves and went to war together. Around the Huron League, other Iroquoian peoples made their home: the Petun, Neutral, Iroquois, and others. Algonquian tribes were also scattered near the land of the Huron.

Huron government was based on the clans. Clan members within each village selected the chiefs who represented them in councils. Each of the eighteen to twenty-four villages in the league was governed by two separate councils: the war council and the civil council. Made up of all the war chiefs and proven warriors of each clan group, the war council met in the longhouse of the most distinguished leader. Daily affairs, such as hunting, fishing, farming, defense, religion, and ceremonies, were discussed by a civil council. This council was led by a chief who was respected for his wisdom and skill as an **orator**.

The Huron had many difficulties with the nearby Iroquois tribes.

Older men, usually at least thirty years old, could attend and speak at this council.

Council members discussed matters at length, listening carefully to opposing viewpoints until everyone agreed on a decision. Any man who wanted to speak was allowed to do so. Individual clans could refuse to take part in an attack on an enemy or other action with which they disagreed. The councils lacked the authority to carry out decisions so they tried to arrive at a consensus, or general agreement.

Each tribe, or nation, was represented by a council of the head chiefs from each of the clans. These clan chiefs met in the tribal council at least once a year. Any chief of a clan could request a tribal council when an issue arose that went beyond the interests of his village. Messengers traveled to each village to announce the meeting, and the chiefs came together. After an exchange of greetings and occasionally gifts, the chiefs seated themselves by village. The chief who had called the meeting then laid the matter before the council in the form of a request for advice. The discussion was highly ritualized. Each speaker first summarized all the previous arguments to assure himself and everyone else that all had been clearly understood. As with village councils, the chiefs strived to reach a decision through consensus.

At least once a year, councils of the four nations of the confederacy were held to renew and strengthen the bonds of friendship, as well as to decide how to deal with enemies. Each village sent clan chiefs, with one serving as spokesman and the others as advisors. The chiefs were seated according to clan and village. Conducted in the same manner as the tribal councils, the chiefs discussed matters concerning the confederacy, but no decision was binding. The Huron League served primarily as a defensive alliance. Due to the long deliberations and emphasis on general agreement, the confederacy was seldom truly unified. Tribes could not be forced to take part in a war or defend a village. When their very survival was threatened in the 1640s, the Huron League could not respond promptly and decisively to the intensive onslaughts of the Iroquois.

Still, the Huron developed thriving communities that lasted for hundreds of years. Their beliefs, rituals, and customs varied from nation to nation, but all were rooted in tradition and widely celebrated. Their alliances brought many people together and ensured the survival of the Huron for generations.

Guerrier Iroquois

Problems with Iroquois warriors eventually led to the Huron leaving their homeland.

This old photograph shows Huron Native Americans dressed in Western clothing.

CHAPTER THREE

Let your nature be known and proclaimed.

—Huron saying

LIFE IN THE HURON NATION

The Huron were mostly a peaceful people who wished to preserve and protect the world around them. They used only what they needed and treated nature and all around them with respect. Believing that each object they encountered had a spirit, the Huron were careful to do what they could to ensure nature was kept safe and only used when necessary.

As generations passed, the Huron continued to live in harmony with the universe. People understood themselves and their place in the world through a knowledge of daily tasks and divine powers. With no written language, they relied upon their remarkable memories to ensure that the lessons of Earth flowed from one generation to the next. Their way of life was recounted through stories and renewed through a complex system of religious beliefs. It is how they as individuals, families, clans, and tribes came to understand the wonder of birth, the trials of youth, and the joys of marriage, as well as the journey toward old age and death. This awareness was passed on whenever a mother placed her newborn in a cradleboard, a man taught his son to make a bow, a woman showed her daughter how to plant corn, and an old man spoke to a group of children gathered around him.

The Life Cycle

The Huron viewed themselves as one with the animals, the plants, and Earth itself—as well as the sun and the stars in the skies above them. They counted the days, months, and years by the cycle of the moon. In the spring and summer, the men left their villages to trade and wage war, while the women tended their green fields. During the autumn, the women gathered wild fruits and hemp in the forests while the men left again, setting up camps and fishing in the rivers and lakes. Later in the season, the men hunted until the winter snows deepened around them, after which families came together again, settling around the warm fires in their longhouses. As recounted in *Jesuit Relations*, their life was shaped through "the seasons of the year by the wild beasts, the fish, the birds, and the vegetation."

When their children were small, the Huron kept them in cradleboards, such as this.

Just as their daily life followed the seasons, so did their view of themselves as belonging to families and clans. There were many beliefs and rituals honoring the cycle of life at birth, coming-of-age, marriage, old age, and death.

Being Born

The Huron rejoiced at the birth of a child, especially a girl who could potentially increase the number of people in the village. Yet parents desired both girls and boys because children were needed to help support them in old age and defend them against enemies.

There were also superstitions regarding pregnancy. It was believed that a woman heavy with child could bring either good or bad luck. Her pregnancy might prevent her husband from finding game. If the woman looked at an animal being stalked by her husband, it would get away. If she ate with people, they would become ill. If she entered the dwelling of a sick person, the condition would worsen. Yet by her very presence she could aid in the removal of an arrow.

When a woman was about to give birth, a corner of the longhouse was partitioned with animal skins. Sometimes, an old woman served as midwife, but experienced women gave birth by themselves and seldom rested after having a baby. A woman might be carrying a load of wood from the forest or be working in a cornfield when she went into labor. She would rise to her feet immediately after giving birth, and once the baby was placed in a cradleboard, she would resume her work. To prove her courage and set a good example for others, the woman did not cry out during labor—although many women died during childbirth.

Sometimes, the mother made her baby swallow grease or oil shortly after birth to ensure good health. With a fish bone she then pierced the newborn's ears, placing a feather quill in the opening. Later, she hung beads from the lobes and around the baby's neck. The Huron kept a supply of names which were not being used by another person in the village. These names were available for the parents to choose from. Perhaps the baby would be given a name with great meaning, such as *yocoisse* (wind), *sondaqua* (eagle), or *taihy* (tree).

Wrapped in furs or skins, the baby was placed in a cradleboard decorated with paintings and strings of beads. Soft down from a reed was used as a diaper, with an opening left in the swaddling through which the baby could make water. During the day, the mother carried the cradleboard on her back or propped it up in the longhouse or outside so her baby could watch her as she worked. During the night, the baby slept naked between the mother and father.

The mother breastfed her baby for two to three years. While the baby was still nursing, she began to feed it bits of meat that she had chewed. Eventually, the child would be able to eat solid foods.

Growing Up

The Huron deeply loved their children and rarely disciplined them. Although allowed a great deal of freedom, children were encouraged through praise and scolding to contribute to the good of the community.

The Huron made their canoes out of birch bark.

Expected to be tough as well, they did not wear a lot of clothing, even in winter, to ensure sturdy bodies in later life. From an early age, children were given chores around the longhouse. Young boys and girls helped weed the fields and chase birds away from the ripening corn.

As they grew up, boys learned to master working bows, arrows, spears, and other weapons. They also competed in many games, such as snow snake, in which they slid a curved stick as far as possible over the snow. These games helped them to build the skills as well as the strong friendships they would need as warriors and hunters. They also learned to make tools, **birch bark** canoes, and longhouses.

Mothers placed a stick in the hands of their young daughters so they might learn how to pound corn from an early age. Girls fetched water and firewood, helped cook meals, and cared for younger brothers and sisters. Following the example of their mothers and the other women in the longhouse, they learned to do household chores, tend crops, tan deerskins, shape clay pots, and weave baskets, some of the many skills they would need when they had a family of their own.

Maturity

When a girl had her first menstrual period, she cooked her food separately in a little pot—as she would whenever she had her period again. The young woman was then considered ready to have a lover or to be married. The Huron did not discourage women from entering into relationships outside of marriage.

At puberty, a young man sometimes went on a vision quest. Venturing alone into the forest, he fasted and drank only water for as long as sixteen days in the hope that his guardian spirit would appear to him. The spirit would help him choose the right path in life. Throughout a man's life, these spirits often reappeared in dreams to offer advice. During times of danger, a man also appealed to his guardian spirit for help.

Marrying

When a man wished to marry a woman, he painted his face and put on his finest ornaments. He presented her with gifts such as a **wampum** necklace, bracelet, chain, earrings, or a beaver robe. If she accepted the presents, he slept with her for three or four nights. If the couple liked each other and the family consented to the marriage, they held a feast in honor of the couple. The father announced the marriage and if there were no objections, there was a feast. Everyone ate stew made of dog, bear, moose, deer meat, or fish. The couple was considered married when the feast ended.

Many young men did not have wives, or *aténonha*, but simply lived with companions known as *asqua*. Whether married or not, men and women were free to have relations with others in the village. If an unmarried woman became pregnant, her lovers came together, each claiming to be the father, and she simply chose the lover she liked best to be her husband. If a married couple did not get along, they were free to leave each other. Although divorce was very common, it happened less frequently when the husband and wife had children.

The Huron would place their dead on high platforms, such as these.

Dying

When a person died, friends and family lamented the loss. The deceased lay on a mat within the walls of the village, and speeches were made in his or her honor. After three days, the people held a feast in which the soul of the deceased took part. Gifts were lavished on the deceased, his family, and those who had arranged the funeral. The body was then placed on a scaffold about 10 feet (3 m) above the ground, along with food, tools, and other belongings needed on the journey to the land of the spirits. If the person had drowned or frozen to death, the body was burned. Babies less than a month old were buried near a path in hopes that their spirit would rise and enter the womb of a woman passing by.

People mourned for ten days, but the spouse of the deceased grieved for one year. During this time, the spouse could not remarry or take part in any feasts. Every eight to twelve years, the entire village held a funeral ceremony known as the Feast of the Dead. The women recovered the bones of any relatives who had died in the previous decade. They scraped the bones clean and wrapped them in furs, after which there were several days of feasting and gift-giving. People told stories about their departed relatives, and the bones, along with personal belongings, were buried in a large pit.

The Huron believed a person had two souls. After death, one floated near the body until it was released at the Feast of the Dead. This soul could be reborn in a name-giving ceremony. The other soul journeyed along a path toward the setting sun and the village of the dead. The soul had to pass a rock in the land of the Petun, where the Oscotarach, or head-piercer, drew out the brains. The soul next had to traverse a log over a turbulent river guarded by a vicious dog. After many months, the soul finally arrived at the village of the dead, which was much like that of the living. The souls of children and the very old who could not make the arduous journey went to another village, where they tended abandoned cornfields.

Providing Food

During much of their early history, the Huron wandered the northern forests and provided for themselves through hunting and gathering. Later, they learned the art of farming and gradually settled in villages. They grew corn and began to cultivate beans, squash, and sunflowers. Individuals and families claimed plots of land near the village, but these fields could not be inherited or sold. The land belonged to them only as long as they worked it.

When new ground had to be cleared, groups of men first chopped down small trees with stone axes. Some of the branches were used as firewood and building materials. The remaining brush was allowed to dry for a while. Then it was heaped around the stumps and burned, the ashes returning some nutrients to the soil. The men girdled, or cut a swath of bark, around the trunks of trees too large to cut down. Sap could no longer flow up the trunk and the trees died, dropping their leaves and allowing sunlight to reach the ground. Clearing the ground was difficult work; several years were required to carve a new field from the dense forest. The women planted around the stumps of the large trees until they decayed and the men could break them apart. To clear old fields that had not been farmed for a number of years, the men simply cut down and burned off any brush that had sprouted since the land was last cultivated. The Huron eventually cleared and farmed all the land around their villages.

Once the men had prepared the fields, their work there was done for the season—the women were responsible for the long months of planting, tending, and harvesting the crops. In the spring, they selected the best corn kernels for seeds and soaked them in water. With wooden spades, they scraped the soil into small mounds, or corn hills. With digging sticks, they made small holes in the mounds, dropped in as many

This photograph shows a Huron Native wearing traditional headgear.

as ten kernels, and covered them. As the clumps of corn plants sprouted, they scraped more soil around the roots. When the corn was several inches tall, women planted beans and squash in some of these hills. The vines of the beans wound up the corn stalks, and the broad leaves of the squash kept the weeds down. Women also planted sunflowers, usually in separate fields. Occasionally, men grew tobacco in small patches near their longhouses, but most often they traded for this sacred plant. They used tobacco in rituals—through the rising smoke they communicated with the spirits—or they simply enjoyed a good smoke.

Over the warm summer months, the women weeded and watered their fields—the very survival of the village depended on their bringing in a good crop. The Huron feared a late frost in the spring and an early autumn frost and a drought during the growing season. They often sought the help of spirits or called upon a medicine man who was thought to have the ability to influence the weather. Children helped the women vigilantly guard the fields from a host of hungry creatures, especially marauding raccoons and flocks of blackbirds. In late August, as the colors turned in the surrounding forests, they harvested their crops. Sliced and dried, squash kept well for several months, as did the beans, which hardened in their pods. However, corn was by far the most important crop grown by the Huron. Some of the corn was shelled and stored in bins or underground pits. The husks pulled back, ears were also hung in bunches from the rafters, away from mice.

When they weren't working in their cornfields or longhouses, women harvested many wild foods and plant materials. They picked strawberries, raspberries, blackberries, blueberries, and wild cherries as each came into season. The berries were eaten fresh or dried for the winter and used to flavor corn soups and breads. Women also gathered wild grapes, dug bulrush roots, and collected acorns and walnuts from the forest floor. They found mussels along the lakeshore and caught turtles in the nearby marshes. In the late summer, they stripped basswood bark, which they boiled, shredded, and made into rope. After the winter storms had knocked dead limbs from the trees, they hauled huge amounts of the wood to the village, where it was needed to cook meals and keep longhouses warm.

While the women tended the crops and gathered foods, the men hunted and fished. In the spring, they caught sturgeon, pike, catfish, sucker, and walleye in the streams and shallow waters along the lakeshore. Sometimes they fished with bone hooks, but their lines often broke, so they relied on nets, wooden spears with barbed bone points, and underwater traps made of wooden slats, called weirs. Poised quietly on the bank or in their birch bark canoes, they speared larger fish. The men scooped up small, schooling fish in dip nets or caught them in weirs. They placed the weirs near the mouths of creeks along spawning runs. The fish would swim into the wide opening and become trapped as the weir gradually narrowed. In the autumn, groups of men journeyed to the islands of Georgian Bay for whitefish, lake trout, and lake herring. During this month-long fishing season, they set up bark cabins and lived in camps away from the village. In the evening, they stretched long **seine** nets with wooden floats and stone weights in the water. In the morning, they drew the seine together, trapping large numbers of fish. During the bitterly cold winter, they occasionally netted fish through holes chopped in the ice.

The men hunted deer, moose, bears, rabbits, muskrats, woodchucks, and beavers, as well as ducks, geese, turkeys, and other birds. The only taboo was eating the flesh of the crow. The Huron killed beavers for their meat and valuable fur with snares, arrows, and clubs. By the 1630s, most of the beavers were gone from Wendake. Dogs were occasionally sacrificed during feasts or eaten

The Huron ate many animals, but not the flesh of crows.

during the lean winter months. However, bears and especially deer were the most common sources of meat. Groups of men used specially trained dogs to stalk bears, whose meat was prepared for feasts. They hunted deer with bow and arrow, or caught the fleet-footed creatures in snares and traps. However, a village most often organized a communal hunt, or drive, in which a large number of people, including women and children, spread out in the woods. They steered the frightened deer over river bluffs or into V-shaped fences where the animals were cornered and easily shot with bow and arrow. Deer were hunted for both their meat and their hides, which were made into clothing or traded with the French and other Native peoples.

Cooking

Women cooked all the meals for their families, usually over the fire pit in the longhouse. They boiled soups and stews in pots and roasted meat and fish. Corn, which comprised about three-quarters of the Huron diet, was included in most meals. Dried and shelled, the kernels were ground between two stones or pounded in a hollowed-out log with a wooden pole about 7 feet (2.1 m) long. The coarse yellow meal was added to soups and made into unleavened breads. Women formed the dough into small cakes, which they wrapped in cornhusks and baked under hot ashes.

Sagamité, (sa-GA-mi-tay) a cornmeal soup, was a favorite among the Huron. Slices of fish, meat, or squash were often tossed into the pot of sagamité. At feasts, a thick corn soup was usually served. A special soup was made from roasted corn kernels mixed with

RECIPE

SAGAMITÉ

Sagamité, which means water or warm gruel, was a traditional cornmeal soup, the staple of the Huron diet. To make the soup, women boiled cornmeal in clay pots—about one part cornmeal to nine parts water. Sometimes, women tossed chunks of meat or fish into the cooking pot as well.

Over time, the name sagamité came to apply to any number of soups, stews, and other Huron dishes. Today, a sagamité recipe with deer meat and kidney beans is served as a dinner meal on the Wendake reserve near Quebec. Here is a basic recipe without meat that you might try as a hot breakfast cereal.

INGREDIENTS

1.5 cups (355 milliliters) cornmeal

0.5 tablespoons (7.4 mL) salt

5 cups (1.2 liters) water

1 cup (237 mL) blueberries

1 tablespoon (14.8 mL) butter

Sugar

Milk

Mix the cornmeal with 1 cup (237 mL) of cold water, then add 4 cups (946 mL) of boiling water, salt, and butter. Cook in the top pan of a double boiler for about 25 minutes or until the mixture has thickened. Place equal amounts of the sagamité in bowls and sprinkle with blueberries or other fruit. Serve with sugar and milk. Serves four or more people.

beans and *leindohy*, immature ears of corn fermented for several months in stagnant water. Leindohy was considered a delicacy. Beans, which were dried and stored in bark or wooden containers, were also eaten, along with squash—especially in the late summer and autumn. The Huron garnished dishes with sunflower oil and rubbed the oil on their bodies and in their hair. Fruits, nuts, and maple syrup were sometimes added to soups and stews. Especially during times of famine, acorns were eaten, but only after they had been boiled repeatedly to remove their bitter taste.

During the hunting season, meat was plentiful but still not a major part of Huron meals. Meat was smoked and mainly served during feasts. Fish was eaten more often. It was sometimes fresh but usually had been smoked or dried where it had been caught. Larger whitefish were sometimes boiled and the oil skimmed off and stored in gourds. One fish known as *einchataon* (possibly catfish) was hung to dry high in the rafters where smoke lingered in the longhouse. Occasionally fish were gutted, but often they were cooked whole with bones, scales, and insides intact.

Except during feasts and times of abundance, the Huron ate twice a day—early in the morning and in the evening. However, a cooking pot was always simmering over the fire, and people could eat whenever they were hungry. They did not wash their hands, but if they were greasy, they simply wiped them on a nearby dog.

Clothes and Accessories

Women made all the clothing for their families, mostly from soft **buckskin**, moose hides, or beaver pelts. Many of the hides came from their own hunting, but some were acquired through trade. Buckskin clothing was usually fringed and often painted with red or brown designs. Robes were trimmed with porcupine quills dyed bright red.

During the warm months, men wore only a buckskin **breechcloth** and moccasins made from deer, beaver, or bear. As winter set in, they donned leggings and long-sleeved shirts and wrapped themselves in beaver cloaks. Many men also wore a fire pouch in which they carried tobacco, pipes, charms, and other belongings. Pipes were especially prized, and men never came to a meeting without having a smoke. Men dyed their hair and wore it in a variety of styles—mostly long but also short or in what is known today as a Mohawk. They often stuck feathers in their hair or wrapped an eel or snakeskin around their head.

In the summer, women wore only a knee-length buckskin skirt and moccasins. In cold weather, they draped a mantle over their shoulders and added a fur robe. Women wore their hair long, with one braid hanging down the back and tied with a strip of leather. For dances, they oiled and dyed their hair, then wrapped a tuft with an eel skin band.

Wampum—tubelike beads made from seashells—was pierced and strung to create jewelry. Both men and women adorned themselves with highly prized wampum bracelets and necklaces. Women also wore earrings and belts of wampum, porcupine quills, or bone.

Both men and women often painted, oiled, and greased their bodies and hair. They mixed minerals or dyes from plants with sunflower oil or animal fat and painted designs on their faces and bodies—red and black were favorite colors, but they also used green and violet.

Arts and Crafts

The Huron did not make handicrafts for trade but only those needed in the longhouse and village. When villagers packed up and moved, they often left their household goods behind.

Along with raising children, tending crops, gathering firewood, cooking meals, and managing the longhouse, women crafted objects essential to their lives. They scraped and softened deer and other animal skin into supple leather for clothing, game bags, and tobacco pouches. They wove mats of reeds and corn leaves, which they placed over doors and on sleeping platforms in the longhouse. Women also wove baskets from reeds and birch bark and sewed pieces of birch bark together to shape cups and bowls. They wove fibers into small textiles, including scarves, collars, and bracelets worn by both men and women.

Women made all the household pottery. First, they dried and crushed the clay dug from a riverbank. Next, they mixed in a little powdered rock to strengthen the clay then added a small amount of water. After shaping a mound of clay into a ball, they punched a hole in the middle with their fist. With their fingers and a small wooden paddle, they gradually formed the pot into a globe, with a narrow opening and low rim. To harden the clay, the finished pot was dried in the sun and baked in an open fire. Women made pots in many sizes—from a few inches to a foot or more in diameter. Cooking pots were made in three sizes, for individuals,

Women were skilled in making crafts such as pottery.

families, and village feasts. Small diagonal, vertical, or horizontal lines were scratched near the lip of the pots. When cold, the pots could not hold water for very long before the clay began to soften. However, they could be used for cooking over a fire.

Smoking pipes were also made from clay—most likely by the men. They shaped the moist clay around a knot of grass, which burned away when the pipe was fired. A small number of highly skilled potters specialized in fashioning pipes. They took greater care in making pipes than pots—better clay was used and the pipe was more evenly fired. Before firing the pipe, potters sometimes rubbed grease over the object to blacken the surface. With round or flared bowls, pipes were often decorated with human or animal figures. Pipes were highly prized, especially those made by the most talented potters, and often used as **barter** in a trade.

During the summer, men also built or repaired the longhouses and palisades. Through this work, along with the clearing of fields, men pushed back the forest and created a reasonably safe area around the village. Men also used the time between the busy fishing and hunting seasons to make canoes or repair old ones. Many of these tasks were undertaken cooperatively, often by all the able-bodied men in the village. To construct a canoe, they carefully formed the ribs from white cedar so the vessel would be balanced and float gracefully in the water. They sheathed this frame with birch bark cut in the spring when the bark was easily peeled from the tree. They sewed the birch bark pieces together with cords and joined them to the frame by weaving a strip of cord along the edge of the canoe. To make the canoe watertight, they boiled pinesap and sealed the seams with the sticky pitch, which hardened into a tough substance called resin.

During the winter, men kept busy in the warmth of the longhouse. They skillfully wove light yet sturdy fishnets. They carved wooden bowls, spoons, and ladles. Occasionally, they made ladles from antlers, using the shapes of the points to suggest a duck in flight. The men fashioned snowshoes and sleds and made clubs and bows and arrows for hunting and warfare. They made points for their arrows from chert, a kind of flint for which they traded. Men also made spear points, awls, and needles from bone. From granite and other hard stones they chipped the heads for axes and adzes.

Sometimes, they carved pipes from stone and made ornaments, such as tube-shaped beads, from bird bones. They also worked seashells into disk-shaped beads and whittled combs and little amulets from bone.

Warring

Like the forest and the clearing, warfare and peace were two opposing forces that had to be balanced within Huron society. So, the village and the tribe had separate chiefs and councils for waging war against hostile peoples and maintaining friendly relations with others. When trading with neighbors, the Huron forgave slights and injuries, but warriors confronted their enemies beyond the clearing with great bravery— and no mercy.

For hundreds of years before the French ventured into the upper reaches of North America, the Huron, as well as other Iroquoians and the Algonquians, had been engaged in raids against hostile villages. The Huron fought the Petuns, possibly the Neutrals, and the five tribes of the Iroquois League, especially the Senecas. In fact, the war with the Iroquois had gone on for half a century. The Huron had also established a network of trade alliances with the Algonquians of Ontario and Quebec and other tribes in the region. These tribes, in turn, fought or traded among themselves or with others, resulting in a complex web of relationships—either hostile or friendly—among all the peoples between the St. Lawrence River and the western Great Lakes.

Like other Iroquoian peoples, the Huron went to war primarily for blood revenge and prestige. In the 1640s, as the fur trade began to change their lifeways, the Huron started to fight other tribes over hunting and trapping territories. Each year, leaders who had proven themselves in battle planned and organized war parties—usually in the late spring or summer. The warriors always gathered in secret for fear of spies within their villages. They dreaded the possibility of informers in their midst and often exiled visitors from the village or even tortured and killed them. Huron chiefs befriended members of neutral tribes and even recruited some of their enemies as spies in the hope that they would warn them of any attack on their villages.

Before war was waged, a great feast was held and the war party excitedly set off for enemy country in birch bark canoes. Five to six hundred warriors took part in these raids; in later years even larger war parties were formed. Each warrior sheathed his chest, arms, and legs in armor made of tightly laced sticks. Armed with war clubs, knives, and bows and arrows, he carried either a long, cedar bark shield or a small disk of tough, boiled leather into battle. Around his head, the warrior wore a circular ornament of red moose hair and his finest jewelry. It was believed that if he was pursued, he could throw down these valuables and the enemy would stop to gather them. Each warrior also brought along a bag of roasted cornmeal—enough to last two months, if necessary.

The warriors might lay siege to an Iroquois village for as long as a week. Once they had killed and captured a number of people, they retreated to Wendake. The following year, the Iroquois might retaliate in similar fashion. Most often, however, when the party reached enemy territory, the warriors broke

The People and Culture of the Huron

into groups of five or six and scattered in the woods around the villages. They ambushed small, isolated groups of people as they fished or worked in the fields, killing or capturing men, women, and children. Some daring warriors slipped into the village at night and terrorized people as they slept. If possible, warriors brought back their enemies' heads or scalps to dry and hang in the longhouse during wartime.

However, a captive was the greatest prize; warriors sought to bring back as many as possible. Some captives, especially women and children, were adopted by families who had lost a relative in war. Most, however, were submitted to a merciless ordeal and then killed. Not only the warriors but women and children thirsted for revenge. Everyone took part in an enemy's highly ritualized torture and slow death. Captives were told to sing during their agony. If they cried out or otherwise failed to display great courage, they and their tribe would be shamed. During the ritual, torturers became increasingly fierce and cruel as they tried to break their victims. Similarly, when Huron warriors were captured and tortured, they were expected to be unflinching—to stand as a symbol of their people.

Wandering and Trading

Men journeyed throughout Huronia on foot or by canoe to hunt, trade, and wage war. During the winter, they wore snowshoes, or *agnonra*, strung with animal gut for trudging through the deep snows. The Huron also fashioned a sled, or *arocha*, with boards of white cedar for hauling goods over the ice. For river travel, men favored small, swift, light canoes paddled by one or two men. Swinging the canoe over his shoulders, a man could easily tote this light craft around rapids or along portages from one stream to another. The Huron relied on large canoes, up to 30 feet (9.1 m) in length, to carry people and goods over great distances. They paddled these canoes over the broad waters of Georgian Bay and the many lakes around Wendake. Since the birch bark sheathing of these canoes was easily damaged, the men always paddled within sight of the shore.

The Huron often traveled to trade with other tribes—they rarely bartered among themselves. They won respect and approval in the village by acquiring wealth and generously sharing it with others. They bestowed gifts at name-giving ceremonies, burials, and during feasts and festivals. They scorned anyone who hoarded goods—a stingy person could be accused of witchcraft and banished.

They traded only with those tribes with whom they had established a peace agreement and a military alliance. Because of long-standing hostilities with the Iroquois, the Huron never bartered with these tribes. Once the Europeans arrived, the Huron wanted to trade with them as well, as long as the Iroquois were not also trading with them. In negotiating to trade furs with Samuel de Champlain, for instance, the Huron insisted that the French first prove their friendship by participating in raids against the Iroquois.

To maintain good relations with their allies, the Huron made every effort to prevent insult or injury to members of allied tribes, especially murder, which would ignite bloody warfare between tribes. Clans and

The People and Culture of the Huron

villages kept a treasury of goods from which they made large payments to the family of a murder victim. A chief could also dip into the treasury to arrange treaties and exchange prisoners, the size of the payment depending on how highly the Huron valued trade with that partner.

The Huron established far-reaching trade routes from their base at the southern tip of Georgian Bay—north to James Bay, east to the St. Lawrence River, south to the Susquehanna River in present-day Pennsylvania, and west to Lake Michigan. The man who discovered a new route held rights as its owner, as did his family members or "those who held his name." His family shared in his trade, while unrelated people had to offer gifts to the rights holder. Those who owned the trade routes often amassed great wealth and became prominent chiefs in their villages. Anyone caught encroaching on a trade route was severely punished. However, if he safely made it back to the village, he would not be harmed. Similarly, the Huron ruthlessly guarded their trade routes from the Petuns, Neutrals, and other tribes outside the confederacy. Anyone who wished to cross their territory had to first seek permission. Otherwise, there would be war.

Men often traded for adventure. As in warfare, they proved their courage by embarking on a dangerous journey. The Huron loved games of chance and sometimes acquired goods for gambling. However, they traded primarily for desirable objects that could be ritually given away, thereby enhancing their prestige within the village. Among the most highly valued goods were shells for making wampum that had made their way from far-off Chesapeake Bay, chert from the

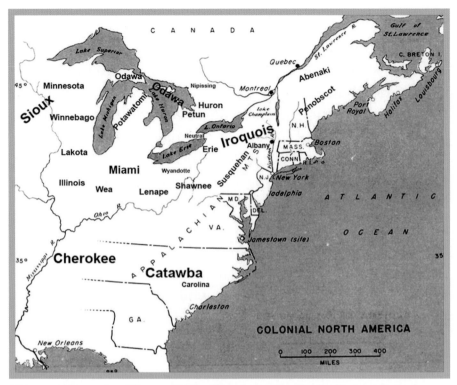

This map shows the different Native American tribes in the Eastern United States in the seventeenth century.

neighboring Petuns and Neutrals, native copper from the shores of Lake Superior, and tobacco. In their cold climate, the Huron could grow little tobacco, so they obtained as much of the sacred plant as possible from the Petuns and Neutrals, and later from the French.

The Huron acquired black squirrel pelts from the Neutrals, made them into cloaks, and traded them to the Algonquians. From the Ottawa the Huron obtained dried berries, mats, fish, and furs in exchange for wampum, nets, and pigments. In addition, the Huron traded pots to Ojibwe living on the eastern shore of Lake Superior and cornmeal to the northern tribes. Many traders were active in this network, which

The People and Culture of the Huron

only expanded with the fur trade. The French clearly admired the bargaining skills of the Huron and eagerly formed a partnership that grew into an international trade, especially in beaver pelts. At the height of the fur trade, as many as three hundred Huron regularly traveled to the St. Lawrence River, and one year, seven hundred men made the journey.

The men, women, and children of the Huron developed extensive communities with prosperous trade and hunting networks. They established relationships with other Huron communities as well as neighboring tribes and fur traders from Europe. As the years passed, more and more Europeans would come to their region, and not all of them would bring peace. Before then, however, the Huron enjoyed the freedom of the lands, the alliances, and the thrill of adventure that accompanied their tribal lifestyle.

The Huron lived close to nature.

CHAPTER FOUR

[There are among the Huron] men who presume to command the rains and winds.

—Jesuit Relations

BELIEFS OF THE HURON

A s they settled in the region, the Huron formed beliefs about the world around them. They had stories to explain the beginning of the world, how humans came to be, and their religious practices. Throughout the centuries, the Huron's beliefs became an important part of life. Some of these customs, celebrations, and rituals are still practiced by Huron members today.

The Huron respected all life, especially the animals that fed and clothed them.

A Living Earth

The Huron believed that everything on Earth, whether living trees or inanimate rocks, had a spirit. The more powerful of these spirits—the sun, the moon, and the sky—were known as **oki**. The sky was an especially vital force, being the source of the weather and the waves on the sea, both of which were divine. The Huron made offerings of tobacco and even sacrificed captives to please and honor the sky. After the sky, the most powerful spirits were Aataentsic, for the moon, and her son (or grandson in some stories) Youskeha, the sun. Certain men, such as medicine men called shamans and great warriors, were also considered oki, as were charms that had proved to be effective.

Since animals had spirits, the Huron also honored them. They never burned their bones or fed them to their dogs. While fishing, they prayed and offered tobacco to the spirit of the waters. Some spirits were seen as human, or partly so. Ondoutaehte, the spirit of war, could be a dwarf or an old woman. Onditachiaé, the spirit of thunder, lightning, and rain, might appear in the form of a human or a wild turkey.

The Huron enjoyed telling stories about their gods. The following is a story about Aataentsic and Youskeha:

> Aataentsic was the moon, and Youskeha was the sun. Both governed the world. Youskeha was responsible for the living—the plants, animals, and people. It was also Youskeha who brought sunshine and rain when needed and other things that helped the people. In contrast, Aataentsic ruled the land of souls and brought death to people.
>
> Although gods, Aataentsic and Youskeha lived as other people but with such an abundance of corn that they had many feasts. Though they dwelled far away, they also often came to the feasts and festivals in the villages of the Huron. At one of these joyful occasions, Aataentsic was badly abused and insulted. Youskeha blamed a horned oki named Tehonrressanden, but later everyone learned that it was actually Youskeha who had abused Aataentsic—his own mother.

Despite his misdeed, Youskeha was still respected by the Huron, while Aataentsic remained resentful of Youskeha who brought much good to the world. At one time, all the water was held under the armpit of a frog. Youskeha slit the armpit, and water flowed over Earth, forming much-needed rivers, lakes, and seas. From the wise turtle, Youskeha learned to make fire, and he generously shared this knowledge with the people.

Similarly, Youskeha once kept all the animals of the world in a great cavern. However, he wanted them to multiply and spread over the land, so one day he freed them. He shot each in the foot with an arrow— all except the wolf, who nimbly dodged the arrow. Because of Youskeha's generous act, the forests abounded in game, and the Huron had good hunting. However, the men have always had difficulty hunting the elusive wolf.

Youskeha also influenced the harvests of corn. If his spirit was glimpsed in the fields, thin as a skeleton and carrying a stunted ear of corn, the people knew they would not have a good crop that year. Yet if he was seen to be in good health, the Huron knew they would harvest much corn.

While Youskeha cared for the living, Aataentsic often undid his helpful deeds. One year, she brought a plague to the villages, and as she journeyed through the longhouses, the people asked her, "Why do you make us die?"

She wrongly blamed her son. "It is because Youskeha is angry at men. They only make war and kill each other. To punish them for their cruelty, he has decided to make them all die." However, when he became old, Youskeha always renewed himself in a moment and became a young man again. He never died. Through the ages the two powerful spirits of Youskeha and Aataentsic battled, seemingly as opposite as life and death yet one never really separate from the other.

Illness, Healing, and Dreaming

The Huron did not build special lodges for religious ceremonies. Like the Iroquois, however, they had a number of healing societies. The members of these groups inherited their powers, received them in a dream, or obtained them through recovery from an illness.

The members of some healing societies crawled around the patient in animal skins or danced in straw masks. Known as Awataerohi, the most prominent society held the Dance of Fire to heal the afflicted. They called upon powerful spirits as they chewed hot coals and sometimes spat them on the patient. Although the system of beliefs within the community was quite complex, religion was also a highly personal matter. Whether shamans, warriors, or traders, individuals were empowered through a vision or by acquiring a powerful companion spirit.

The Huron had an intricate system of beliefs about preventing illness and curing the sick. They believed that illness came not only from natural causes but also from evil spirits and unfulfilled wishes. People suffering physical illnesses or injuries were treated by a shaman with herbal remedies. Wild sarsaparilla was given for wounds and Indian turnip roots for head colds. If the patient did not get better, the Huron believed the sickness must have a supernatural cause.

Many Native American tribes, including the Huron, had shamans, or medicine men, who sometimes dressed in animal skins before healing a patient.

A shaman, or ontetsan, treated people suffering from illness of both the body and spirit through magic, feasts, dances, and spells. He usually removed one or more offensive objects from the person's body—a

The People and Culture of the Huron

tuft of hair, an animal claw, or perhaps a feather.
He touched or shook the patient, then symbolically
displayed the object. It was sometimes believed that a
witch had cast a spell over the person, so the shaman
tried to find the witch. Once found, if the witch could
not remove the spell, he or she might be executed if
the chief or council so ordered.

If the patient was suffering from unfulfilled wishes,
the medicine man interpreted his or her dreams. Then
he asked the patient's relatives to help fulfill these
unsatisfied desires.

Celebrations

The Huron loved to host feasts and festivals at which
guests sang, danced, and ate heartily. Usually held during
the late autumn, winter, or early spring, these gatherings
were an important way to strengthen friendships and to
improve one's social status within the village.

Every winter, many people in the village took part
in a three-day festival known as **ononhouaroia**, or
"the upsetting of the brain." Most often, the event
was triggered by the illness of a well-known person.
A group ran through the village, loudly shouting,
acting crazy, and telling the inhabitants of each
longhouse, "We have dreamed." They didn't reveal
what had been dreamed, only hinted through riddles
until they received the desired objects. This ritual not
only provided a reason for gift-giving, but the Huron
believed that it helped to protect the well-being of
everyone in the village. At the end of the festival the
participants went into the woods to "cast out their
madness" in hopes that the ill person would get better.

During feasts, the host was respected because he freely shared his wealth and good fortune. There were four kinds of feasts: *enditeuhwa*, to offer thanksgiving; *awataerohi*, to cure a sick person; *athataion*, for a dying person to say farewell to his close friends; and *atouronta ochien*, to sing in preparation for war, to honor a man who wished to be renowned, or to give the name of a deceased chief to another person. At some gatherings, known as *anondahoin*, only tobacco was smoked. People arrived at feasts in their finest clothing and ornaments. They carefully styled their hair and often painted their faces and bodies. Inside the longhouse, the guests sat on mats or cedar boughs spread on the ground or on the platforms.

Shaking tortoise-shell rattles, two chiefs led the singing. They stood in the midst of the dancers, who formed a loose oval around them. The feast might last all day or several days. Food was served in the morning and afternoon when the host announced, "*Nequarre!*" ("The kettle has boiled!") The guests joyfully responded, "*Ho!*" and struck the ground or platform. Along with singing, dancing, and eating, these gatherings were enlivened with games and contests.

Playing Games

Like feasts and dances, games were part of the *onderha*, the foundation of social life among the Huron. The Huron loved to play games and gamble. Good luck in gambling was believed to come from supernatural forces. Whether between individuals or teams of villagers and neighbors, no contest was ever held without a lively wager, and the stakes were often high. Men were known

The People and Culture of the Huron

The Huron played many games, including a version of lacrosse.

to gamble away everything they owned—even their clothing. Gambling was not always a happy time. Often, it led to angry fights and even murder.

The three favorite games were stickball, the dish game, and *aescara*. Known by most Native peoples around the Great Lakes, these games were played to cure sickness and prevent disaster. The Huron also competed at stickball to bring good weather or to honor a dead player. Played with a ball and sticks in a field near the village, this early version of lacrosse was a rough game, a kind of war game with frequent injuries in which young men proved their courage. The dish game was played with five or six fruit stones or small pottery disks painted black on one side and white or yellow on the other. Sitting in a circle, people took turns putting the stones in a wooden bowl and then striking the bowl on the ground. One side won when all the

People attached feathers to cobs of corn to make darts.

The People and Culture of the Huron

stones fell out with the same color facing up. Women also played the dish game, but they held the stones in their hands and dropped them on an animal hide stretched on the ground. Little is known about *aescara*, except that one player held three or four hundred white reeds. Another player snatched a handful of reeds and then guessed how many reeds his opponent still held.

Through their experiences, the Huron's cultural identities developed. They formed tight bonds within their village and were brought together in times of feasts, festivities, and illness. Although sometimes their measures were strict, the Huron's beliefs were honored and celebrated in each community.

This photograph shows a group of Huron-Wendat from Wendake, circa 1880.

Samuel de Champlain possibly encountered members of the Huron tribe on his expedition to North America.

CHAPTER FIVE

In the 1600s, Europeans would transform Huron culture, identity, and history forever.

OVERCOMING HARDSHIPS

In the early 1600s, the Huron's world changed forever with the arrival of Samuel de Champlain, a French explorer known for founding New France—later Canada—and the province of Quebec. Champlain's arrival signaled the entry of many French citizens—mostly fur traders—into Huron territory. While at first the Huron were interested in establishing trading relationships with them, their attitude changed when more immigrants came to settle in the region. It became clear as the years passed that these newcomers would transform Huron culture, identity, and history in ways they could not have imagined.

Early French Relations

At first, relations were good. Huron leaders initially met with the French and started lucrative trading partnerships. They would exchange beaver pelts for European goods, including cloth, glass beads, knives, and kettles. At the time, beaver hats were the height of fashion in Europe, and demand for the pelts was great. Because of their geographic location and experience as traders, the Huron were ideally located to serve as middlemen in what became known as the Great Huron Trade Circle. The Huron obtained European goods from the French, which they in turn traded—along with their own corn—to their neighbors, including the Petun, Neutral, Ottawa, Algonquian, and Nipissing, for beaver pelts. Beavers were plentiful where these Native people lived. Then, the Huron returned to their homes and traded the beaver pelts to the French.

This relationship led to other problems, however. As they traded and came to understand more about the Europeans, the Huron began to desire European goods. Soon, the Huron came to depend upon metal tools and household objects, including pots, skillets, and kettles. They also began to rely on guns as weapons. They soon lost the knowledge and skills to make clay pottery and buckskin clothing, as well as their own tools and weapons. The demand for furs was also so intense that they had less time to grow food for themselves, let alone surplus corn, beans, and squash to trade with their northern and western neighbors and the French.

Before long, the Huron encountered other challenges. The first were missionaries who entered

Jesuit priests arrived in the 1600s to convert Native tribes such as the Huron.

Huron villages. Known as **Black Robes**, the Jesuits attempted to convert Native people to Christianity. Because the Huron had settled in villages, the Jesuits believed that they would be easier to approach and convert than the migrating tribes. However, the deeply personal beliefs of the Huron differed markedly from those of Christianity. For many years, the Huron resisted efforts to force them to abandon their traditional beliefs. Then, between 1635 and 1640, smallpox and measles epidemics swept through Huron villages, reducing the population to just ten thousand people. Unable to understand the devastation or find a cure, many Huron turned to Christianity as a last refuge. Others blamed the missionaries for bringing the disease to their villages, and conflict arose between these two factions.

Eventually, the Black Robes were able to influence and change the Huron way of life. The following is a song by Father Jean de Brébeuf (1593–1649) that blends traditional Huron life with the Christmas story. Composed by Father Brébeuf in the Huron language in the 1600s, the song was passed down from the 1600s through generations of converted Huron people before being translated into French and English.

The Huron Carol

'Twas in the moon of the wintertime
When all the birds had fled,
That mighty Gitchi Manitou sent
angel choirs instead;
Before their light the stars grew dim
and wond'ring hunters heard the hymn:
    "Jesus, your King, is born,
    Jesus is born. *In excelsis gloria!*"
Within a lodge of broken bark
The tender babe was found.
A ragged robe of rabbit skin
Enwrapped His beauty 'round;
And as the hunter braves drew nigh
The angel song rang loud and high:
    "Jesus, your King, is born,
    Jesus is born. In excelsis gloria!"
The earliest moon of wintertime
Is not so round and fair
As the ring of glory

Many Huron eventually converted to Christianity and built churches, such as this one.

On the helpless infant there.
The chiefs from far before Him knelt
With gifts of fox and beaver pelt.
"Jesus, your King, is born,
Jesus is born. In excelsis gloria!"
O children of the forest free.
O sons of Manitou.
The Holy Child of earth and heaven
is born today for you.
Come kneel before the radiant Boy
Who brings you beauty, peace, and joy.
"Jesus, your King, is born,
Jesus is born. In excelsis gloria!"

Overcoming Hardships

The Huron battled with the Iroquois and eventually were pushed from their homelands.

Attacks and the Aftermath

Weakened by disease and internal conflict, the Huron were attacked in the early 1640s by the members of the Iroquois League to the south—Mohawk, Oneida, Onondaga, Seneca, and Cayuga tribes. The Iroquois had established a similar trading partnership with the

The People and Culture of the Huron

Dutch of New Amsterdam (later New York), and they wanted to trade with the same northern tribes with whom the Huron had been exchanging beaver pelts. Armed with Dutch guns, Seneca warriors attacked villages in 1648, and a year later, devastated by war, disease, and starvation, the Huron abandoned their territory. Many, including most of the Tahontaenrat clan, merged with the Onondaga and Seneca tribes, which had also lost many people.

Others, whose descendants are still known as Huron, or Wendat, migrated to the island of Gahoendoe in Georgian Bay. However, there was little farmland on the island and the largely Christian group was encouraged by Jesuit missionaries to move to Quebec and settle among the French in 1650. The next year about four hundred Huron left Quebec and settled on Ile d'Orléans in the St. Lawrence River. Their population grew to five or six hundred within the next five years, but seventy-one people were killed in a Mohawk attack in 1656, after which the Huron sought peace with the Iroquois League. The Attignawantan clan joined the Mohawks, strengthening their declining population, and the Arendahronon became part of the Onondaga. The Onondaga, however, betrayed the agreement and killed all the Huron men and took the women and children as captives.

About two hundred Attignawantan stayed in Quebec. For the next forty years they sought a home, moving to Beauport on the St. Lawrence River in 1667 and then to Côte St.-Michel. In 1673, their population having grown to three hundred people, they migrated to Ancienne Lorette, where they lived for twenty-four years. As their population grew, they had to move again, in 1697. This time they moved to Jeune Lorette, 8 miles (13 km) north of the city of Quebec, where they became known as the Huron of Lorette. The sandy soil there was not suitable for agriculture and when the Huron lost hunting and fishing territory in 1701, they began to support themselves by making traditional crafts—moccasins, snowshoes, and canoes—and selling them in nearby Quebec. The Huron received additional lands, including 1,352 acres (547 hectares) known as Quarante Arpents in 1772 and 9,600 acres (3,885 ha) known as Cabane d'Automne in 1851. They leased and later sold the parcels of land so they could continue to specialize in traditional handicrafts. Today, with a population of around than 1,500 people, the Hurons still operate their businesses on the Wendake Reserve, although many have adopted a French-Canadian style of life. The reserve also serves as a tourist site, educating people of all ages about the Huron way of life from centuries ago to today.

After the Iroquois wars, another group of Huron moved southwest, just 26 miles (42 km) away, to live among the Petun and the Neutral—their former trading partners. However, they enjoyed only a few years of peace. Toward the end of 1649, the Iroquois again attacked and drove them from their new homes. They became wanderers—through what is now Michigan, Wisconsin, Ohio, and Illinois. They first settled on the island of Michilimackinac (mish-ul-lee-MACK-uh-nack), now known as Mackinac Island, in Michigan, and then Huron Island, which was later named Rock Island, near Green Bay, Wisconsin. Others moved near Detroit, Michigan, and then northern Ohio.

Along the way, the Huron-Petun traded and hunted with other mostly Algonquian-speaking peoples, as well as fought against other tribes. While in Detroit, the Huron-Petuns became trading partners with the British, who came to refer to them as the Wyandot.

However, most Wyandot continued to ally themselves with the French, especially since the British were allied with the Iroquois. When the French lost the French and Indian War (1754–1763) and surrendered their territory in North America, the Wyandot continued to fight the British. Led by Pontiac, a great Ottawa chief, an alliance of tribes that included the Wyandot attacked Detroit, Fort Pitt, and Sandusky. During the American Revolution (1775–1783), however, the Wyandot sided with the British. After the American Revolution ended, they faced a new enemy— Americans pushing westward. In the early to mid-1800s, the Wyandot settled in Ohio and east of the Mississippi River. However, by 1843, they had sold all these lands and moved to Indian Territory in the fork of the Kansas and Missouri Rivers in what is now Wyandotte County, Kansas. They purchased land there from the Delaware, or Lenape, people.

In 1855, a Wyandot delegation negotiated a treaty with the United States government that provided for allotment, or distribution, of their lands to tribal members. Each individual received a parcel of the land that had once belonged to the group. However, the tribe as a whole lost its identity. The Wyandot who received land became United States citizens but surrendered their tribal membership. The Wyandot also suffered prejudice from settlers and were often cheated out of their land.

They fell into deep poverty and in 1867, many people moved to the northeastern part of Indian Territory in present-day Oklahoma where the Seneca, their former enemies, gave them refuge. The Seneca eventually granted over 20,000 acres (8,094 ha) of land to the Wyandot on the north side of their reservation.

The United States government upheld this agreement with the Seneca, and this small group of Wyandot, numbering about 110 people, were soon joined by others who had lost their land in Kansas. They formed a government with annual meetings and the election of first and second chiefs and council members. On the eve of Oklahoma statehood in 1907, Wyandot lands were again allotted with the surplus lands to be sold to settlers. This time, some tribal members were not even included in the allotment process, although the United States Congress had promised to purchase lands for them elsewhere. Some Wyandot went to Ohio, and others returned to Canada, where they were again known as the Huron and where they live to this day.

In 1937, the Wyandot reorganized under the Oklahoma Indian Welfare Act of 1936. However, in 1956, the United States embarked upon another termination process, which not only ended federal assistance but threatened the very existence of the Oklahoma tribes, including the Wyandot, with the loss of their land. The Wyandot were allowed to retain their governments, but without land they had no way to remain together as a people. By the late 1960s, it became obvious that the termination plan was a disaster, as Native peoples not only lost land but also a sense of community and identity as a people. Today, the Wyandot have regained their status as a federally recognized tribe. Their headquarters is at Wyandotte, Oklahoma. In recent years, Huron tribes have done much to preserve their cultural identity and history. They have successfully encouraged people to attend summer schools and powwows. They likewise manage their own websites that maintain up-to-date information about the tribe and their activities. Online language classes preserving Huron words, phrases, and dialects, are also offered. It is important to all Huron members that their heritage be remembered and shared throughout the generations with as many people as possible.

Developing Language

Originally, the Huron spoke a dialect of the Iroquoian language family. However, as the years passed, the language began to evolve. The Jesuits reported in the 1600s that the Attignawantan and Petun tribes spoke the same language, but the Attignawantan and Tahontaenrat tribes spoke slightly different versions. Because of their prominence in trade in the early 1600s, the language of the Huron was adopted by the French and a number of Algonquian-speaking peoples who lived around the Great Lakes. However, when the Huron were devastated and dispersed, their language and culture became threatened. It is believed that the last fluent speaker of the language in Canada died in 1912. Today, most Huron in Canada speak French while the Wyandots living in the United States speak English. Recent efforts have been made to preserve the Huron way of speaking, though. Many tribes have language lessons taught in their schools, or they promote online classes where people can sign up to learn the language.

The following words and phrases are drawn from *An Ethnography of the Huron Indians, 1615–1649* by Elisabeth Tooker. The original sources are the *Jesuit Relations* and the accounts of Recollect friar Gabriel Sagard-Théobat.

Daily Words and Phrases

agochin	a feast
agnonha	iron person; Huron word for the French
aiendawasti	a polite person
cachia otindion	You are very clever.
chay	good day
chieske	What do I know?
ho, ho, ho	a joyful greeting
ho, ho, ho, outoécti	many thanks
ondayee ihaton onennoncwat	That is what my heart says to me, that is what my appetite desires.
oniondechouten	Such is the custom of our country.
téondion (or tescaondion)	You have no sense.
yo eiouahaoua	Come, put on the kettle.

Spiritual Terms

arondiuhanne (or ahondiuoyissa)	words for a medicine man: "You are people who understand high and supernatural matters."
endionrra	the soul that thinks and deliberates
gonennoncwal	the soul in so far as it bears affection to any object
khiondhecwi	the soul that gives life to one's body
oki andaérandi	like a spirit; the soul possessed of reason

Animals

ahonque	Canada goose
ahouyochetrout	trout
anarisqua	wolf
angyahouiche	turtle
ausquoy	caribou
hixrahon	sturgeon
horhey	swan
ondathra	muskrat
ondettontaque	wild turkey
oraquan	crow

scangaresse	skunk
sconoton	deer
sondaqua	eagle
sondareinta	moose
soruissan	pike
taron	duck
tintian	woodpecker
tioointsiq	snake
tochingo	great blue heron
tsoutaye	beaver

Fruits and Berries

hahique	small fruits in general
ohentaqué	blueberries
poires	pears
tichionte	strawberries
toca	cranberries
tonestes	plums

It is clear that although the Huron suffered many hardships, they overcame them and continue today. Their history, language, and identities are preserved in the members of the Huron tribe today and the efforts of these men, women, and children to ensure their ancestry is remembered. After a long struggle to be identified as a tribe, the Huron have won their battle and continue to be a significant part of the story of the First Peoples of North America.

Today, the Huron remember their ancestry by wearing traditional ceremonial clothing.

Overcoming Hardships

A young man dressed in traditional clothes and face paint dances at the Wendake Powwow in 2012.

*Our ancestors
incorporated storytelling
as a way to pass on
cultural narratives ...
in colder months.*

—Wyandot of Anderdon
website

THE NATION'S PRESENCE NOW

Since the Huron's arrival in North America many thousands of years ago, the nation has changed in many ways. The centuries have brought many successes and more challenges, some of which continue. For a time, the Huron League was among one of the strongest alliances in Native culture; however, before long, Europeans along with their weapons challenged that notion and changed their world forever. Today the many arms of the Huron Nation continue to have significance in Huron society, culture, and history.

At its height, the Huron League was at least twenty thousand strong, although some estimates run as high as forty-five thousand. Today, the number is below ten thousand. Nearly all the Hurons in Canada live on the Wendake Reserve, whereas the Huron-Petuns, known as Wyandots or Wyandottes, are scattered throughout the United States. Some Wyandots live on reservations in Kansas and Michigan.

The Wyandotte Community

Today, the Wyandotte Nation of Oklahoma no longer has a reservation. They live scattered around the United States, but they still own tribal lands near the town of Wyandotte. Enrollment in the Wyndotte Nation is around 5,800, of which 1,200 live near the headquarters in Oklahoma. Nevertheless, there is some debate whether the Wyandotte Nation of Oklahoma is a part of the Huron tradition. According to their website, www.wyandotte-nation.org, they are united through other Huron tribes that later joined theirs, but they themselves are technically not part of the Huron group, as the Huron confederacy had dissolved before the Wyandotte Nation officially began. Due to their later associations, however, this book does consider them part of that tapestry.

Those living in or near the community of Wyandotte are led by their own Wyandot Council. Consisting of a chief, second chief, and four councillors, each elected to a four-year term, the group manages the Wyandot

The People and Culture of the Huron

This sign greets people to the Wendake Huron Reservation.

Tribal Center and oversees federal programs. The council holds monthly meetings at which anyone in the community can voice concerns. There is also an annual meeting in which new members of the council are chosen. Council members are largely concerned with improving the education of Wyandot children and providing better housing for their people, as well as greater employment opportunities. An important goal of tribal leaders is to create greater economic self-sufficiency for individuals living in the community. The Wyandot are also working to improve health care, notably the prevention and treatment of diabetes and heart disease, both of which are prevalent among their population.

In recent years, many improvements have been made to the community. In 2006, 57 acres (23 ha) was granted to the Wyandotte for a housing project, and a grant worth nearly $800,000 was received to help create and construct a preschool on tribal lands. Also that year, ground was broken for the creation of a casino, which opened in 2007. Additionally, in 2007, the tribe acquired 165 acres (67 ha) to construct powwow grounds. In 2008, the Wyandot Tribal Heritage Department opened. This was a significant construction for the community, as it meant the tribe now had a central location to preserve its history and cultural identity. In 2014, the tribe held its twenty-fifth annual powwow, celebrating their heritage and history with traditional dress, dances, and festivities.

The Huron-Wendat Community

During the first half of the twentieth century, the community of Wendake, the reserve near Quebec where the Huron-Wendat (previously the Huron of Lorette) make their home, steadily dwindled—both in population and size. People left the reserve, and leaders sold much of the land. The Canadian government also confiscated some of the land for parks and the national railroad until the Huron had just 26 acres (10.5 ha) in the late 1960s. In 1968, Huron leaders negotiated with the Canadian government, which returned Native lands, and the reserve was enlarged to over 165 acres (67 ha). The Huron also embarked on a number of successful business ventures, and today the people of the Wendake Reserve enjoy one of the highest standards of living of Native peoples in Canada. Many people own their own stores or small businesses, while others commute to jobs in Quebec and other towns. Several people have entered professions as doctors, authors, musicians, and artists. However, many people have devoted themselves to traditional handicrafts for which the people at Wendake are widely acclaimed. During the 1990s they produced three thousand canoes and fifty thousand pairs of snowshoes each year. Today, people live in modern houses along shady streets amid thriving enterprises. Children attend Huron Elementary School from grades one through four, then travel to nearby schools in Loretteville or Quebec.

The reserve is governed by the Huron National Council, consisting of five members elected to two-year terms. Chosen as chief councillor, one member presides over all meetings. The council manages community issues, including health care, and programs funded by the Canadian government. In 2010, the tribe celebrated the 250th anniversary of the signing of the Anglo-Huron Treaty, which protected and preserved some of their rights and tribal lands, and in 2013, the Huron-Wendat joined in commemorating thirty years of relations between the Canadian government and the First Nations of Canada.

Today, some of the Huron-Wendat population lives at Wendake, while others live off the reserve in Canada and the United States. For many years, the Huron have committed themselves to reviving traditional ways of life. One of the ways they have done so is through tourism. Each year, many people visit the historic buildings comprising the town. One of these sites is the chapel of Nôtre-Dame-de-Lorette, a Catholic church

A replica of an ancient Huron village can be seen at the Wendake Huron Reservation.

built at Wendake hundreds of years ago. Another is the Tsawenhonhi mansion, a home built to house Grand Chief Nicolas Vincent Tsawenhonhi in the 1820s. Finally, visitors can get a glimpse into the Wendat's past by visiting the Huron-Wendat Museum, an extensive

The People and Culture of the Huron

organization that preserves and protects the Huron-Wendat ancestry and way of life.

The Wyandot Nations of Kansas and Anderdon

There are two other Wyandot nations, the Wyandot Nation of Kansas and the Wyandot Nation of Anderdon, Michigan. These communities continue to play active roles in Huron society. Both have dedicated websites with information about their tribes, and both try to preserve their heritage and culture through various means and activities. The Wyandot Nation of Anderdon website, wyandotofanderdon.com, for example, has a page focusing on Huron language, genealogy, and Anderdon tribal events.

Although today the Huron and the Wyandot have little contact with one another, they do meet occasionally. In 2015, a meeting of the confederacy chiefs was held in Rockwood, Michigan. Chiefs from

A young boy dances at the Wendake Powwow.

The People and Culture of the Huron

the Wyandotte of Oklahoma, the Huron-Wendat, the Wyandot of Kansas, and the Wyandot of Anderdon communities joined together for a meeting and feast. While this contact is infrequent, their histories remain intertwined. All four communities are descendants of one of the greatest confederacies of Native American history, and all have endured obstacles and hardships at the hands of European and American settlers. They have overcome diseases, threats, and destruction and continue to flourish in today's ever-changing society. As they embark on the future, they will continue to strive for prosperity, well-being, and success. Overall, they will continue to advocate for their heritage, preserving their history, culture, and identity for centuries to come.

The Huron tribes have had many chiefs, including Hen-Tah.

To advance the standard of living of the tribe ... to promote the general welfare ... of the Wyandotte Nation.

—Wyandotte Tribe of Oklahoma mission statement

FACES OF THE HURON NATION

Over the course of the Huron's existence there have been many men and women who have left their mark on the history of the nation. They have been warriors, shamans, traitors, and great leaders. These are some of the people who have had great influence on the Huron Nation.

Adario (Kondiaronk, Sastaretsi, Gaspar Soiaga, Souoias, Le Rat, The Rat) (circa 1650–1701), a leader, diplomat, and speaker, was born a Petun, but his people joined the Hurons after the Iroquois invaded their territory in the mid-1600s. He grew up to become a great chief during the first of the French and Indian Wars. He became a skilled diplomat, especially in playing the French against the Iroquois who were allied with the British. Adario also spoke eloquently in defense of his people's rights.

In 1688, with arms furnished by the French, he led a war party against the Iroquois. On the way, he was told that an Iroquois peace delegation was headed to Montreal. Adario ambushed and captured the Iroquois, telling them that the French had ordered the attack. To show his goodwill, he freed the captives, keeping one hostage to replace one of his men killed in battle. Adario then journeyed to Michilimackinac where the commandant had not yet heard that the Iroquois wished to have peace. There, he ordered the captive to be executed. When he returned to his village, Adario released another Iroquois captured in a previous battle, sending the warrior home with the message that the French had killed the other captive despite the Hurons' efforts to spare him. On August 25, 1689, the furious Iroquois killed hundreds of people in attacks on Montreal and other French settlements along the St. Lawrence River. Adario managed to remain friendly with the French while convincing the Iroquois that he was also sympathetic to them.

In later years, Adario converted to Christianity. He died while heading a peace delegation in Montreal in 1701. The French buried him in a cemetery there with full military honors.

Ahatsistari (Eustache Ahatsisteari) (active mid-1600s), war leader, headed two victories against the Iroquois from 1641 to 1642, early in the wars with their neighbors to the south. In one battle, he led fifty warriors against three hundred Iroquois; in the other, the warriors fought in canoes on Lake Ontario. Not long afterward, a band of Mohawks attacked a French and Huron war party and captured Ahatsistari. He was briefly held prisoner, then killed.

Seven years later, in March 1649, the five tribes of the Iroquois League swept into Huron territory north of Lake Ontario, drove them from their villages, and took over the region.

Leaford Bearskin (1921–2012), chief and pilot, was a formative member of the Wyandotte community of Oklahoma. Born in Oklahoma in 1921, Bearskin grew up to become a beloved leader. He served as a crew chief and pilot in World War II, and following the end of

Leaford Bearskin was a beloved leader of the Wyandotte community.

the war, he continued his military service. He went on to serve in Japan, Korea, and Nebraska. Eventually, he retired from the air force in 1960. In 1983, Bearskin became chief of the Wyandotte Nation. There, he devoted himself to providing a better life for the people of his tribe. During his twenty-eight years as a chief, the tribe saw many improvements for their standard of living, including health care, education, employment, and cultural identity. He resigned as chief in 2011 and was replaced by Billy Friend. In 2012, he passed away, leaving a lasting legacy for the people of Wyandotte, Oklahoma.

Deganawida (Deganawidah, Dekanawida, Dekanawidah, Dekanahwidah; The Heavenly Messenger) (active 1500s), Huron spiritual leader, is believed to have been born near present-day Kingston, Ontario, in the early to mid-1500s. He was one of seven brothers. According to legend, his mother foresaw in a vision that he would cause the Huron people to be destroyed, so she tried to drown him three times in a nearby river.

When he grew up, Deganawida crossed Lake Ontario, allegedly in a stone canoe, and met **Hiawatha**, a Mohawk warrior, in what is now New York State. The two men envisioned a union of the five tribes, which came to be known as the Iroquois League. It is believed that Deganawida, who had a speech impediment, was the visionary and Hiawatha was the spokesman who journeyed among the Cayuga, Mohawk, Oneida, Onondaga, and Seneca. After he had founded the league, planted a Tree of Peace to ensure tranquility among the allied tribes, and written the Great Law

"From his forehead fell
his tresses,
Smooth and parted like
a woman's."
"The Song of Hiawatha."
—Longfellow.

Hiawatha was not Huron, but he and a Huron member,
Deganawida, united five tribes to make the Iroquois League.

that would keep the tribes from fighting, Deganawida
became a Pine Tree Sachem, a leader chosen by merit
instead of heredity. Once the alliance was established,
one story recounts that Deganawida departed in
his stone canoe, vowing to return if the alliance was
ever threatened.

In 1649, the Iroquois attacked and defeated the Huron,
fulfilling the sad prophecy of Deganawida's mother.

Dunquat (Dunquad, Daunghquat, Half-King) (active late 1700s), leader, was a Wyandot, the descendants of the Hurons who migrated to present-day Ohio. He became a leader of allied bands of Wyandot, Shawnee, Ojibwe, and Ottawa warriors that allied with the British during the American Revolution (1775–1783). Dunquat led a series of attacks against American settlements west of the Allegheny Mountains. Serving as a peacemaker among tribes, he also protected the Christianized Moravian Delawares from an attack by another faction. After the Revolutionary War, Dunquat allied with Little Turtle, a Miami chief, and continued to resist westward movement of American settlers. In 1795, along with Little Turtle he signed the Treaty of Fort Greenville, which gave nearly all lands of Ohio and parts of Indiana, Illinois, and Michigan to the United States.

Mary McKee (Tarema or Carrying A Pond) (1838–1922), traveler and advocate for land rights, was a woman remembered for her dedication and ancestry. Born in Michigan in 1838, she was the granddaughter of Chief Quoqua, who had fought with the British during the War of 1812, and the daughter of Thomas McKee, a descendant of Irish immigrants who traded with the Wyandot during the American Revolution. She was five years old when she moved with her family and members of the Wyandot of Ohio to Kansas. Within a few months of their arrival, the Wyandot were dying from lack of housing, flooding, and disease. Mary's father was one of the victims. Not wanting to continue living there, Mary's mother moved her and her daughter to Michigan. Later, Mary would return to Kansas to go to school. Adulthood

The People and Culture of the Huron

was also difficult on her. Once she had finished her studies, Mary went to Wyandotte, Oklahoma, in 1867. She tried for many decades to be granted an allotment of land and pay; however, she only received a $21 annuity (about $350 in 2015). In 1911, Mary became of interest to an anthropologist, Marius Barbeau, who interviewed her about the Wyandot way of life and culture. Sadly, she passed away on June 11, 1922, and her grave was left unmarked until 2003.

This image shows Tarhe, a famous medicine man and leader of the Huron Nation.

Tarhe (Crane, Le Chef Grue, Monsieur Grue) (1742–1818), medicine man, was born near what is now Detroit, Michigan, and became a leader among the Wyandot. He allied with Cornstalk, a Shawnee chief, against settlers at Point Pleasant in Lord Dunmore's War of 1774. Then he fought with Little Turtle at Fallen Timbers from 1790 to 1794. Tarhe played a pivotal role in negotiating the Treaty of Fort Greenville of 1795 and thereafter became an American ally. A friend of Shawnee chief Catahecassa, he opposed Tecumseh's advocacy of resistance against westward expansion. He allied with the Americans during the War of 1812 and fought at the Battle of the Thames in 1813. He died at the age of seventy-six in Crane Town, near the present-day site of Sandusky, Ohio. Many notable people, including the Seneca chief Red Jacket from Buffalo, New York, attended his funeral.

William Walker

William Walker (1800–1874), interpreter, leader, was the son of a white captive, who became a chief of the Wyandot in Ohio, and his mixed-blood wife. Educated among settlers, Walker studied European languages at Kenyon College. He served as private secretary and interpreter for Lewis Cass, the governor of Michigan Territory. Later, he became a source for Henry Rowe Schoolcraft, who studied Native peoples of the Great Lakes region.

When his father died in 1824, Walker became chief of the Wyandot in Ohio. Opposed to removal, he fought for the best possible terms when his people were relocated to Kansas in 1842. He became the provisional governor of the Nebraska Territory in 1853, which was divided into the Kansas and Nebraska Territories the following year.

Walk-in-the-Water (Myeerah) (ca. 1775–ca. 1825), leader, came to support Tecumseh's dream of an

This woman demonstrates the songs and drum of the Huron tribe to which she belongs.

independent nation, although he had signed peace treaties with the United States at Detroit in 1807 and 1808. During the War of 1812, he and Roundhead, another Wyandot leader, allied with the British and proved to be effective warriors. On January 22, 1813, they fought with Colonel Henry Proctor against a force of Kentuckians at Raisin River south of Detroit, Michigan. On October 5, 1813, Walk-in-the-Water also took part in the Battle of the Thames, where Tecumseh was killed. After the war, Walk-in-the-Water made his home near Brownstone, Michigan.

These men and women lived during various periods of history, yet they were all essential to the story of the Huron Nation. Some of them improved the nation, while others brought destruction and devastation. Regardless, they contribute to the rich tapestry of the Native American past and provide context for the Huron today.

CHRONOLOGY

1500s Four tribes unite to form the Huron League.

1534 Frenchman Jacques Cartier encounters Iroquoian-speaking people along the St. Lawrence River, possibly including the Huron.

1609 The Huron encounter the French, most likely explorer Samuel de Champlain, the founder of New France.

1626 The first Jesuits, accompanied by Recollect friars, enter Huronia.

1649 The Huron must abandon their homeland because of the wars with the Iroquois League.

1697 After wandering for half a century, some Huron people settle in Jeune Lorette, north of Quebec, which becomes the Wendake Reserve.

1843 The remnants of one Huron group, known as Wyandot or Wyandotte, arrive in Kansas.

1855 The Wyandotte tribe cedes its land in Kansas City, Kansas, to the United States, except the "portion of land now enclosed and used as a public burying ground," which is today known as the Huron Cemetery.

1867 The Wyandot who choose not to become citizens of the United States are granted a reserve of approximately 20,000 acres (8,094 ha) in what is now Oklahoma.

1937 The Wyandot adopt a constitution under the Oklahoma Indian Welfare Act and become known as the Wyandotte Tribe of Oklahoma.

1956 The United States moves to terminate the Wyandotte tribe and demands that all tribal land be sold.

1968 The Canadian government expands the Wendake Reserve to more than 165 acres (66.8 ha).

1977 When petitioned to reinstate the Wyandotte as a tribe, Congress determines that the Wyandotte was still legally considered a tribe.

2011 Wyandotte of Oklahoma chief Leaford Bearskin steps down and Billy Friend takes his place as chief of the tribe.

2012 Leaford Bearskin dies.

2014 Wyandotte of Oklahoma celebrate twenty-five years of their annual powwow.

2015 The Twelfth Annual Gathering of Wyandotte tribes occurs.

GLOSSARY

Algonquian Native peoples of North America who speak Algonquian languages and, in many cases, share similar customs. All the non-Iroquoian tribes in the Northeast were Algonquian, including some of the Huron's immediate neighbors—especially the Ottawa, the Nipissing, and the Algonquin. Ojibwe, Delaware, Abenaki, and Potawatomi are among the many other Algonquian tribes of North America.

barter To trade. Also, the thing being traded.

birch bark A thin layer of bark from the birch tree that may be fashioned into coverings for canoes, wigwams, and useful household items.

Black Robes A name for the Jesuit missionaries who sought to convert the Huron and other Native peoples in Canada.

breechcloth A cloth or skin worn between the legs and around the hips; also breechclout.

buckskin Deer hide softened by a tanning or curing process.

chasm A large hole.

clan A number of families related to a common ancestor.

confederacy A political union of related tribes, such as the Huron or the Iroquois, for warfare and trade.

fur trade A network through which Native peoples exchanged animal furs, notably beaver pelts, for European goods.

Hiawatha A great Mohawk statesman who helped found the League of the Iroquois.

Huronia The region between Georgian Bay and Lake Simcoe in Ontario that was the homeland of the Huron. Also known as Wendake.

Iroquoian The group or family of languages spoken by related tribes in eastern North America, including the Huron and the six Iroquois tribes.

Jesuit A priest in the Society of Jesus, a Roman Catholic order founded by Saint Ignatius Loyola in 1534.

loam Earth, ground.

longhouse A dwelling of the Huron and other Iroquoian people, consisting of a wooden framework sheathed with elm or cedar bark.

oki Supernatural powers, including the sun and sky, as well as companion spirits of individuals.

ononhouaroia A Huron ceremony, literally meaning "the upsetting of the brain," in which people guessed and tried to fulfill each other's secret dreams.

orator An expert speech-giver.

palisade A defensive wall of upright, sharpened poles surrounding a Huron village.

reservation Land set aside by the United States or Canadian government as a home for a Native American tribe; called a reserve in Canada.

sagamité Corn soup commonly eaten by the Huron.

seine A large net with weights on one side and floats on the other. It usually hangs vertically and is used to catch fish when the ends are drawn together.

sojourn Journey or trip.

swath A long, wide strip of land.

wampum Shell beads in strings or collars used by the peoples of eastern North America as jewelry and as symbols of good faith in treaties.

Wendake The Huron homeland also known as Huronia; also, the home of the modern Huron-Wendat tribe of Quebec.

Wendat The Huron name for themselves, meaning "Islanders" or "Dwellers on a Peninsula."

Wyandot The descendants of the Huron and other tribes who moved to the Great Lakes region and then Ohio before settling in their present home in northeastern Oklahoma.

BIBLIOGRAPHY

Barr, Daniel. *Unconquered: The Iroquois League at War in Colonial America*. Modern Military Tradition. Westport, CT: Praeger Publishers, 2006.

Boyden, Joseph. *The Orenda: A Novel*. New York: Alfred A. Knopf, 2014.

Dunbar-Oritz, Roxanne. *An Indigenous Peoples' History of the United States*. ReVisioning American History. Boston: Beacon Press, 2014.

Garrad, Charles. *Petun to Wyandot: The Ontario Petun from the Sixteenth Century*. Mercury. Ottawa, ON: University of Ottawa Press, 2014.

Gibson, Karn Bush. *Native American History for Kids: With 21 Activities*. For Kids. Chicago: Chicago Review Press, 2010.

Gray-Kanatiiosh, Barbara A. *Huron*. Native Americans. Edina, MN: Checkerboard Library, 2004.

Karich, Grant. *Scugog Carrying Place: A Frontier Pathway*. Toronto, ON: Dundurn Press, 2013.

Labelle, Kathryn Magee. *Dispersed But Not Destroyed: A History of the Seventeenth-Century Wendat People.* Seattle, WA: University of Washington Press, 2014.

McLimans, David. *Big Turtle.* London: Walker Childrens, 2011.

Moore, Christopher. *Champlain.* Toronto, ON: Tundra Books, 2004.

O'Brien, John A. *Saints of the American Wilderness: The Brave Lives and Holy Deaths of the Eight North American Martyrs.* Manchester, NH: Sophia Institute Press, 2004.

O'Malley, John W. *The Jesuits: A History from Ignatius to the Present.* Lanham, MD: Rowman & Littlefield, 2014.

Seeman, Erik R. *The Huron-Wendat Feast of the Dead: Indian-European Encounters in Early North America.* Witness to History. Baltimore, MD: Johns Hopkins University Press, 2011.

Steckley, John L. *The Eighteenth-Century Wyandot: A Clan-Based Study.* Indigenous Studies. Waterloo, ON: Wilfrid Laurier University Press, 2014.

Weidensaul, Scott. *The First Frontier: The Forgotten History of Struggle, Savagery, and Endurance in Early America.* New York: Houghton Mifflin Harcourt, 2012.

FURTHER INFORMATION

Want to know more about the Huron? Check out these websites, videos, and organizations.

Websites

History of the Wyandot of Anderdon: 1600s

www.wyandotofanderdon.com/wp/?page_id=164

This website lists events that happened in Wyandot history during the 1600s.

History of the Wyandot of Anderdon: 1700s

www.wyandotofanderdon.com/wp/?page_id=169

This website lists events that happened in Wyandot history during the 1700s.

Huronia Museum: Wendat Village

huroniamuseum.com/exhibits/huron-village

Learn about the replica Wendat village at Huronia Museum, built to reflect life for Natives from 1500 to 1600.

Ohio History Central: Wyandots

www.ohiohistorycentral.org/w/Wyandot_Indians?rec=646

This site describes what life was like for the last Wyandots to leave Ohio.

Wyandot Language

www.wyandotte-nation.org/culture/language

Learn how to speak some of the Wyandot language by visiting this website. It includes audio clips of some of the most popular Wyandot words.

Videos

The Fall of Huronia

www.youtube.com/watch?v=0Ei6ZcP4WQ8

This video details the arrival of Christianity to Huron territory and the fall of Huronia as a result of disease and warfare.

Samuel de Champlain

www.youtube.com/watch?v=yfRHqWCz3Zw

This video briefly describes the life and exploration of Samuel de Champlain.

Organizations

Bande Indienne de la Nation Huronne-Wendat

255 Place Chef Michel Laveau
Wendake, QC G0A 4V0
Canada
(418) 843-3767
www.wendake.ca

Huronia Historical Parks
Sainte-Marie Among the Hurons
16164 Highway 12 East
Midland, ON L4R 4K8
Canada
(705) 526-7838
www.saintemarieamongthehurons.on.ca

Huronia Museum & Huron Indian Village
549 Little Lake Park Road
PO Box 638
Midland, ON L4R 4P4
Canada
(705) 526-2844
www.huroniamuseum.com

Wyandot Nation of Anderdon
PO Box 68
Trenton, MI 48183
www.wyandotofanderdon.com

Wyandotte Tribe of Oklahoma
64700 E. Highway 60
Wyandotte, OK 74370
(918) 678-2297
www.wyandotte-nation.org

INDEX

Mackinac Island, 84, 104
marriage, 42–43
McKee, Mary, 108–109
Michigan, 21, 84, 94, 99,
    108–111
missionaries, 19–20,
    78–80, 83
    See also Jesuit
moccasins, 53, 84
Montreal, 17, 104

Neutral (tribe), 32, 57,
    61–62, 78, 84
New France, 19, 77
New York, 12, 83, 106, 110

Ohio, 21, 84–86, 100, 110
Ojibwe, 62, 108
oki, 66–67
Oklahoma, 21, 86–87,
    94, 101, 105–106,
    109
Oklahoma Indian
    Welfare Act, 86
ononhouaroia, 71
Ontario, 10, 57, 106
orator, 32
Ottawa (tribe), 62, 78, 85,
    108

palisade, 11, 28–29, 56
Petun, 20, 32, 45, 57,
    61–62, 78, 84–85, 87,
    94, 104
Pontiac, 21, 85
Potawatomi, 20
pottery, 29–30, 42, 50,
    54–55, **55**, 62, 73, 78
powwows, 87, **92**, 96, 100

Quebec, 17, 21, 57, 77,
    83–84, 96–97

Red Jacket, 110
reservation (or reserve),
    21, 84, 86, 94, **95**,
    96–97, **98**
Revolutionary War, 21,
    85, 108

sagamité, 50–51
Sagard-Théobat, Gabriel,
    19, 88
seine, 49
Seneca, 57, 82–83, 86,
    106, 110
shamans, 29, 66, 69, 70–71,
    70, 103
Shawnee, 108–109

ABOUT THE AUTHOR

Raymond Bial has published more than eighty books—most of them photography books—during his career. His photo-essays for children include *Corn Belt Harvest, Amish Home, Frontier Home, Shaker Home, The Underground Railroad, Portrait of a Farm Family, With Needle and Thread: A Book About Quilts, Mist Over the Mountains: Appalachia and Its People, Cajun Home,* and *Where Lincoln Walked.*

As with his other work, Bial's deep feeling for his subjects is evident in both the text and illustrations. He travels to tribal cultural centers, photographing homes, artifacts, and surroundings and learning firsthand about the national lifeways of these peoples.

The emeritus director of a small college library in the Midwest, he lives with his wife and three children in Urbana, Illinois.